Second Workshop on Stylistic Variation 2018

New Orleans, Louisiana, USA
5 June 2018

ISBN: 978-1-5108-6366-8

Printed from e-media with permission by:

Curran Associates, Inc.
57 Morehouse Lane
Red Hook, NY 12571

Some format issues inherent in the e-media version may also appear in this print version.

Printed by Curran Associates, Inc. (2018)

For permission requests, please contact the Association for Computational Linguistics at the address below.

Association for Computational Linguistics
209 N. Eighth Street
Stroudsburg, Pennsylvania 18360

Phone: 1-570-476-8006
Fax: 1-570-476-0860

acl@aclweb.org

Additional copies of this publication are available from:

Curran Associates, Inc.
57 Morehouse Lane
Red Hook, NY 12571 USA
Phone: 845-758-0400
Fax: 845-758-2633
Email: curran@proceedings.com
Web: www.proceedings.com

NAACL HLT 2018

Second Workshop on Stylistic Variation

Workshop Proceedings

June 5, 2018
New Orleans, Louisiana

Sponsors:

THOMSON REUTERS

Introduction

The 2nd Workshop on Stylistic Variation (StyVa) at NAACL 2018 follows up the successful first iteration of the workshop at EMNLP 2017. The goal of the workshop is to offer a venue for bringing together a large but previously underserved and splintered community within computational linguistics, attracting a variety of perspectives on style from traditional areas within NLP, including authorship attribution, author profiling, genre studies, natural language generation, distributional lexicography, and literary and educational applications; to this end we have defined stylistic variation as broadly as possible, to include any variation in phonological, lexical, syntactic, or discourse realization of particular semantic content, due to differences in extralinguistic variables such as individual speaker, speaker demographics, target audience, genre, etc. This spirit of diversity is reflected this year particularly in our first invited speaker, James Pennebaker, whose main research has been published in psychology (though we note that his LIWC lexicon is a standard tool for NLP researchers).

In this iteration, we received 11 submissions, of which we accepted 6 as talks (54.5%); 1 paper was later withdrawn due to acceptance elsewhere and instead of the paper we will have a third invited talk. Even with a smaller set of papers than last year, the topics covered are diverse, including stylistic difference due to social variables, language background, and genre. Perhaps the most striking difference compared to our last iteration was a relative lack of natural language generation papers (we did have one, though!).

We thank the authors for choosing StyVa as a venue for their excellent work, all of our invited speakers (James Pennebaker, Rada Mihalcea, and Barbara Plank) for their invaluable contribution, and of course the reviews provided by our esteemed Program Committee. We'd also want to thank the ACL workshop organizing committee for their support.

We would also like to thank Thomson Reuters for their generous sponsorship of this workshop.

We look forward to a great workshop in New Orleans!
Julian Brooke
Lucie Flekova
Moshe Koppel
Thamar Solorio

Organizers:

Julian Brooke, Thomson Reuters
Lucie Flekova, Amazon Research
Moshe Koppel, Bar-Ilan University
Thamar Solorio, University of Houston

Program Committee:

Nikolaos Aletras (University of Sheffield)
Yves Bestgen (Université catholique de Louvain)
Alberto Barrón-Cedeño (Qatar Computing Research Institute)
Walter Daelemans (University of Antwerp)
Jacob Eisenstein (Georgia Tech)
Roger Evans (University of Brighton)
Alexander Gelbukh (Instituto Politécnico Nacional)
Adam Hammond (San Diego State University)
Graeme Hirst (University of Toronto)
Ekaterina Kochmar (Cambridge University)
Vasileios Lampos (University College London)
Dominique Legallois (Université Paris 3, Sorbonne-Nouvelle)
Manuel Montes-y-Gomez (Instituto Nacional de Astrofísica, Optica y Electronica)
Dong Nguyen (Alan Turing Institute)
Umashanthi Pavalanathan (Georgia Institute of Technology)
Ellie Pavlick (University of Pennsylvania)
Barbara Plank (University of Groningen)
Martin Potthast (Leipzig University)
Vinod Prabhakaran (Computer Science, Stanford)
Daniel Preotiuc-Pietro (University of Pennsylvania)
Emily Prud'hommeaux (Rochester Institute of Technology)
Sudha Rao (University of Maryland)
Maarten Sap (University of Washington)
Andrew H. Schwartz (Stony Brook University)
Anders Soegaard (University of Copenhagen)
Benno Stein (Bauhaus-Universität Weimar)
Joel Tetreault (Grammarly)
Sandra Uitdenbogerd (RMIT University)
Sowmya Vajjala (Iowa State University)
Svitlana Volkova (Pacific Northwest National Laboratory)
Wei Xu (Ohio State Unversity)
Marcos Zampeiri (University of Wolverhampton)

Invited Speakers:

Prof. Rada Mihalcea, University of Michigan
Prof. James W. Pennebaker, University of Texas at Austin
Prof. Barbara Plank, University of Groningen

Table of Contents

Stylistic variation over 200 years of court proceedings according to gender and social class
Stefania Degaetano-Ortlieb 1

Stylistic Variation in Social Media Part-of-Speech Tagging
Murali Raghu Babu Balusu, Taha Merghani and Jacob Eisenstein 11

Detecting Syntactic Features of Translated Chinese
Hai Hu, Wen Li and Sandra Kübler 20

Evaluating Creative Language Generation: The Case of Rap Lyric Ghostwriting
Peter Potash, Alexey Romanov and Anna Rumshisky 29

Cross-corpus Native Language Identification via Statistical Embedding
Francisco Rangel, Paolo Rosso, Julian Brooke and Alexandra Uitdenbogerd 39

Conference Program

Tuesday, June 5, 2018

9:15–9:30 ***Opening Remarks***

9:30–10:30 ***Invited Talk by James W. Pennebaker: Measuring Linguistic Variation with Function Words***

10:30–11:00 **Break**

11:00–11:30 *Stylistic variation over 200 years of court proceedings according to gender and social class*
Stefania Degaetano-Ortlieb

11:30–12:00 *Stylistic Variation in Social Media Part-of-Speech Tagging*
Murali Raghu Babu Balusu, Taha Merghani and Jacob Eisenstein

12:00–12:30 *Detecting Syntactic Features of Translated Chinese*
Hai Hu, Wen Li and Sandra Kübler

12:30–14:00 **Lunch**

14:00–15:00 ***Invited Talk by Rada Mihalcea: What Does Language Tell us about the People Behind it***

15:00–15:30 *Evaluating Creative Language Generation: The Case of Rap Lyric Ghostwriting*
Peter Potash, Alexey Romanov and Anna Rumshisky

15:30–16:00 **Break**

16:00–17:00 ***Invited Talk by Barbara Plank: Author Profiling from Text and Beyond***

17:00–17:30 *Cross-corpus Native Language Identification via Statistical Embedding*
Francisco Rangel, Paolo Rosso, Julian Brooke and Alexandra Uitdenbogerd

Stylistic variation over 200 years of court proceedings according to gender and social class

Stefania Degaetano-Ortlieb
Department of Language Science and Technology
Saarland University
66123 Saarbrücken, Germany
s.degaetano@mx.uni-saarland.de

Abstract

We present an approach to detect stylistic variation across social variables (here: gender and social class), considering also diachronic change in language use. For detection of stylistic variation, we use relative entropy, measuring the difference between probability distributions at different linguistic levels (here: lexis and grammar). In addition, by relative entropy, we can determine which linguistic units are related to stylistic variation.

1 Introduction

Understanding language/stylistic variation[1] according to social variables (such as gender, age or social class) is of great interest to sociolinguistics (Eckert, 1989; Labov, 1963; Bernstein, 1971; Tagliamonte, 2006) and has recently received increased attention in the NLP community for developing methods able to predict social context based on language use (see Nguyen et al. (2016) for an overview).

In this paper, we take a diachronic perspective and study how language use in court proceedings changes over a time span of approx. 200 years considering the interaction between gender and social class. A major focus is on female of higher class, as we hypothesize that as the inferior social position of women was increasingly questioned from the mid-nineteenth century, this might be reflected in their language use[2]. For this, we use the Old Bailey Corpus (Huber et al., 2016), a diachronic corpus of manually socio-linguistically annotated data of court proceedings raging from 1720 to 1913 (see Section 3.1). We apply an information-theoretic approach using relative entropy, which has been successfully applied for the analysis of diachronic variation in language use investigating the development of written scientific English (cf. Degaetano-Ortlieb et al. (to appear); Degaetano-Ortlieb and Teich (2016)).

We make two major contributions: First, we investigate change in language use showing how groups of gender and of lower vs. higher social class change linguistically over time. This contributes not only to (historical) sociolinguistics but also to the NLP community strengthening awareness of accounting for stylistic variation and diachronic change in language use. Second, rather than selecting predefined features to analyze stylistic variation, we use whole linguistic levels (lexis and grammar) as described in Section 3.2 from which stylistic features can be inferred.

After introducing related work (Section 2) as well as our data set and methodology (Section 3.2), we test our hypothesis of change in language use for female of higher class investigating stylistic variation (Section 4). Section 5 concludes the paper with a brief summary and an outlook on future work.

2 Related Work

Traditional sociolinguistic approaches on variation (Eckert, 1989; Labov, 1963; Milroy and Milroy, 1985; Milroy and Gordon, 2003; Tagliamonte, 2006; Trudgill, 1974; Weinreich et al., 1968) work with surveys and relatively small but detailed manually collected data. Variation is analyzed considering single as well as several social variables at a time, but the small sample size affects generalization of the findings.

Increasing data availability of naturally occurring text has lead to analyze sociolinguistic variation also in corpus- and computational linguistics, especially within the social media domain (see

[1] We use stylistic variation in the sense of the workshop, i.e. variation of linguistic levels based on extra-linguistic variables (here: social variables and time).

[2] see also https://www.oldbaileyonline.org/static/Gender.jsp

Proceedings of the 2nd Workshop on Stylistic Variation, pages 1–10
New Orleans, Louisiana, June 5, 2018.

e.g. Eisenstein (2015); Eisenstein et al. (2011); Nguyen et al. (2015); Danescu-Niculescu-Mizil et al. (2013); Jurafsky et al. (2009)). Recently, also the possible interplay between social variables is considered (Prabhakaran and Rambow, 2017), but is mostly confined to age and gender (see e.g. Ardehaly and Culotta (2015); Argamon et al. (2007); Barbieri (2008); Burger et al. (2011); Eckert and McConnell-Ginet (2013); Holmes and Meyerhoff (2003); Hovy and Søgaard (2015); Nguyen et al. (2014); Peersman et al. (2011); Schwartz et al. (2013); Wagner (2012)) as other social variables – such as social class – are not easily available (cf. Sloan et al. (2015)).

In fact, the gap in coverage of other social variables has recently lead to a full strand of research focusing on determining and analyzing income through Twitter content using a wide range of features. Preotiuc-Pietro et al. (2015a) use word clusters and embeddings to predict occupational class of Twitter users. Preoiuc-Pietro et al. (2015) apply non-linear methods for regression using besides shallow textual features (e.g. average no. of tweets) also user profile and psycho-demographic features (e.g. no. of followers, gender, age) as well as emotion features (e.g. positive/negative sentiments). Hasanuzzaman et al. (2017) are the first to use user cognitive structure in terms of the user's overall temporal orientation to predict income uncovering a correlation between future temporal orientation and income.

While the above mentioned literature is devoted to social media giving valuable insights into sociolinguistic, behavioral and social science research of the *present*, in this paper we study *diachronic* change in language use of social groups in approx. 200 years of court proceedings.

Considering the linguistic levels at which variation according to social variables is analyzed, in sociolinguistic approaches the phonological level prevails, while in computational approaches the lexical level is often reported to be best in prediction tasks. Other linguistic levels were mostly neglected often due to low performance of NLP tools especially for social media (e.g. sentence parsing). Recent advances in this direction have been made, for example, by Flekova et al. (2016) using besides surface features (e.g. length of tweets), readability features (such as the Automatic Readability Index or Gunning-Fog Index) as well as several style features (such as explicitness, no. of hedges) also syntax features by means of parts of speech.

In our study we are dealing with transcribed spoken utterances from the court, i.e. spoken English in a relatively formal context, thus we can consider besides lexical features also grammatical features approximated by part-of-speech trigrams. Our lexical features include content as well as function words, thus lexical as well as grammatical features will both reflect stylistic variation.

Relative entropy as a measure of divergence between corpora has been already applied successfully for the analysis of written scientific English from the 17th to the present (Degaetano-Ortlieb et al., to appear; Degaetano-Ortlieb and Teich, 2016; Degaetano-Ortlieb and Stroetgen, 2018) and for intra-textual variation, more precisely variation within sections of research articles (Degaetano-Ortlieb and Teich, 2017).

3 Data and Methods

3.1 Old Bailey Corpus

The court proceedings of the Old Bailey Court in London contain transcribed utterances of the court's trials spanning from 1674 to 1913. According to Emsley et al. (2018) the City of London "required that the publisher should provide a "true, fair and perfect narrative" of the trials" and "witness testimony is the most fully reported element of the trials". Thus, the utterances in the proceedings are arguably a relatively precise account of spoken English of that period.

The Old Bailey Corpus (OBC; Huber et al. (2016)) is built from a digitized version of the proceedings and spans from 1720 to 1913. It represents a balanced subset of the proceedings with semi-automatically identified utterances. Each utterance was semi-automatically annotated with sociolinguistic information based on sociobiographical speaker data found in the context of the trials. For this, an annotation tool was developed that first automatically detected speakers based on a list of 7,500 male and female first names (approx. 95% coverage) and in a second step allowed to scroll through the data to annotate sociobiographical information. Witnesses, for example, had to begin their statement by mentioning their profession (cf. Huber et al. (2016)). The OBC amounts at approx. 14 million spoken words (around 750,000 words per decade). It is part-of-speech tagged with CLAWS 7 (with reported accuracy of 95-98%) and sociolinguistically annotated for speaker information (gender, age, occupation according to the HISCO standard), social class (HISCLASS standard), speaker role (defendant, interpreter, judge, lawyer, victim, and witness), and textual information (scribe, printer, publisher). In addition, the corpus is divided up into years, decades and periods of fifty-years. The corpus is encoded in the Corpus Query Processor (Evert, 2005) and available for download[3] or on the CQPweb platform[4].

For the analyses, we consider the sociolinguistic annotations of gender (female, male) and social class (higher, lower) as well as the fifty-years time periods[5]. To control for speaker role, as there are no female judges or lawyers, we confine our data set to the roles of victim and witness. Table 1 gives an overview on the token size of each subcorpus.

period	FH	FL	MH	ML
1700	49,142	47,497	286,322	185,862
1750	121,942	170,090	1,084,068	855,178
1800	135,887	217,224	2,499,314	1,422,027
1850	168,246	217,830	4,069,475	1,317,113
1900	61,518	63,494	1,158,354	294,608

Table 1: Subcorpus sizes of the OBC confined to speaker role witness and victim

3.2 Detection of stylistic variation across social variables

For detecting stylistic variation, we use the method described in Fankhauser et al. (2014) based on relative entropy, precisely Kullback-Leibler Divergence (Kullback and Leibler, 1951). This approach allows us to compare probability distributions by measuring the number of additional bits needed to encode a (sub)corpus A with an optimal code for a (sub)corpus B.

$$D(A||B) = \sum_i p(unit_i|A) log_2 \frac{p(unit_i|A)}{p(unit_i|B)} \quad (1)$$

To control for differences in vocabulary size, the corpora are represented by means of unigram language models which are smoothed with Jelinek-Mercer smoothing and lambda 0.05 (cf. Fankhauser et al. (2014) and Zhai and Lafferty (2004)).

Here, we use relative entropy to measure the difference between language use of female and male of higher and lower class over time in bits. Thus, we compare four groups (female higher class (FH), female lower class (FL), male higher class (MH) and male lower class (ML)) over five time periods (1700, 1750, 1800, 1850, 1900). For each comparison (i.e. comparison between two groups, e.g. FH vs. FL 1700, FH vs. FL 1750, etc.) a relative entropy (language) model is built. We then compare the relative entropy values obtained for each comparison to determine differences in language use across social variables and time. The higher the relative entropy value of a comparison, the more apart the two groups are and vice versa.

Note also that Kullback-Leibler Divergence is an asymmetric measure, i.e. a comparison of FH vs. FL 1700 does not necessarily result in the same relative entropy value as a comparison of FL vs. FH 1700. For comparison of variation in language use, the asymmetry is useful as it allows us to account for the directionality of the comparison.

For each comparison, we also obtain the individual unit's weight, i.e. how much a unit contributes to the difference. For example, comparing FH vs. FL 1700, we obtain the additional bits needed for a unit in FH based on the unit's probability in FL:

$$D_{unit}(FH||FL)_{1700} = p(unit|FH) log_2 \frac{p(unit|FH)}{p(unit|FL)} \quad (2)$$

The higher the relative entropy value of a unit, the greater the unit's contribution to the difference, i.e. the more distinctive the unit is for a given group in a time period. In addition, for each comparison we test for significance of the relative frequency of a unit in the two groups by an unpaired Welch's t-test (threshold of a p-value<0.05):

$$t = \frac{mean_{FH} - mean_{FL}}{\sqrt{(\frac{var_{FH}}{n_{FH}} + \frac{var_{FL}}{n_{FL}})}} \quad (3)$$

with var denoting the variance and n the number of documents in a group (cf. Fankhauser et al. (2014)).

To consider differences at the lexical level, the units for the relative entropy models are words. To approximate the grammatical level, we use part-of-speech (POS) trigrams as units.

In comparison to other corpus-linguistic approaches, such as classification (e.g. Teich et al.

[3] http://www1.uni-giessen.de/oldbaileycorpus/

[4] https://corpora.clarin-d.uni-saarland.de/cqpweb/usr/index.php?thisQ=accessDenied&corpusDenied=obc2&uT=y

[5] 1700: 1700-1749; 1750: 1750-1799; 1800: 1800-1849; 1850: 1850-1899; 1900: 1900-1920.

(2016)) or correspondence analysis (e.g. Glynn (2014)) just to mention a few, relative entropy directly measures the divergence between two groups in bits of information. The contribution of each unit to the divergence provides valuable insights into which units are distinctive for each group.

4 Stylistic variation across gender and social class

We investigate stylistic variation considering the interaction between gender and social class at two linguistic levels (lexis and grammar). Our focus is on change in language use of female higher class. Women's social position was increasingly questioned in the mid-nineteenth century. We hypothesize that this movement might be reflected in a change in language use of female higher class when compared to female lower class as well as male higher and lower class. As appropriate, we will also compare diachronic tendencies of the other groups.

Our concrete research questions are the following: (i) Is there a difference in language use between female higher class compared to female lower class and male higher and lower class, (ii) if so, which lexical and grammatical units contribute to these differences, (iii) do these differences change over time?

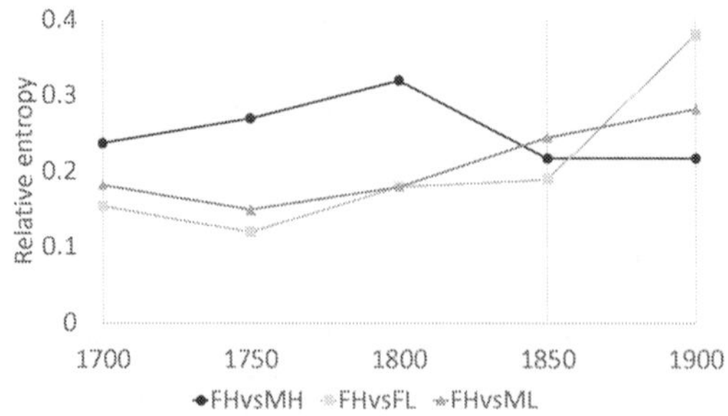

Figure 1: Relative entropy across fifty-years time periods in the OBC for female higher class (FH) vs. the other groups

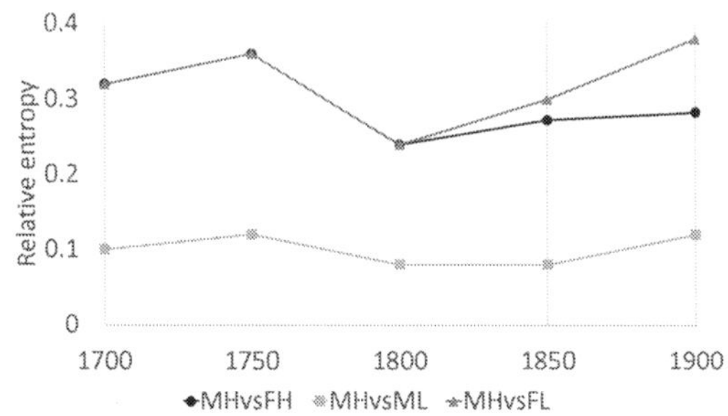

Figure 2: Relative entropy across fifty-years time periods in the OBC for male higher class (MH) vs. the other groups

4.1 Lexical level

At the lexical level, we compare each group by relative entropy using words. From Figure 1, we can see that from 1700 to 1800 relative entropy between female higher class (FH) vs. female and male lower class (FL and ML) is lower (below 0.2 bits) than vs. male higher class (MH) (above 0.2 bits with a slight increases to 0.3 towards the period of 1800). Thus, for female higher class around 0.8 to 0.15 additional bits are needed in comparison to male higher class than from the lower class. After 1800 this changes, based on words FH becomes less distinct to MH (towards 0.2 bits), while it becomes more distinct from the lower class (vs. ML 0.2825 bits, i.e. 0.065 more bits than FHvsMH, and vs. FL 0.38 bits, i.e. 0.17 more bits than FHvsMH, in the period of 1900).

Let us compare this to male higher class (MH) vs. the other groups. From Figure 2, we see how relative entropy of MH vs. ML is relatively low (around 0.1 bits). Compared to female (FH and FL) relative entropy is higher, especially in 1700 to 1750 (i.e. around 0.2-0.25 more bits). Towards 1800 relative entropy of MH vs. FH and FL decreases. After 1800, relative entropy remains stable for MH vs. FH, while MH vs. FL increases.

Comparing Figure 1 and 2, we can see how relative entropy reflects quite well the difference related to the communicative experience of language users. Compare, for example, FH vs. MH (Figure 1) and MH vs. FH (Figure 2) in 1900 (0.2825 bits for MH vs. FH and 0.2175 bits for FH vs. MH). Here relative entropy differs due to the asymmetry of Kullback-Leibler Divergence, which allows us to model differences depending on the directionality of the comparison. Thus, if a language model of male higher class is used to predict language use of female higher class, we obtain a lower relative entropy value than vice versa. Intuitively this means that male of higher class can better understand female of higher class (here: based on words), while female of higher class need more effort (more bits) to understand male of higher class.

Let us now consider which units (here: words) contribute most to the attested differences. Consider the comparison between female higher class (FH) vs. female lower class (FL). How is the increasing difference as depicted by relative entropy (see again Figure 1) reflected in the use of words? For this, we inspect the contribution of each word to the difference (as described in Section 3.2) and visualize this in a word cloud (using the visualization approach by Fankhauser et al. (2014)). The size of the word denotes its contribution by relative entropy (in bits), the color denotes relative frequency of each word in a time period (from red for high relative frequency to blue for low relative frequency). From these clouds, we can detect variation in terms of words indicating lexical as well as stylistic differences.

As for lexical differences, FL speak distinctively about authorities (*sir, master, mistress, mr, mrs*) and objects (*door, kitchen, bedside*) related to the household; FH use distinctively business oriented vocabulary (*counter, penny, profit, purchase, business*) and words for persons related to either marriage (*husband, wife*) or crime (*officer, prisoner*).

Considering stylistic differences, while FL distinctively use personal pronouns (e.g. *his, I, me, he, him*) and verbs (e.g. *carry, become, wash, work, coming, went, going*), FH in comparison to FL over time develop a pronounced nominal style with distinctive use of nouns, definite determiners (*a, an*), and prepositions (*of, in*). Thus, female lower class use increasingly an involved verbal style over time, while female higher class make use of a nominal more informational style when compared to one another (cf. Conrad and Biber (2001, 28) for involved vs. informational production).

4.2 Grammatical level

While stylistic differences can already be seen when considering the lexical level, we consider grammatical structures approximating them by part-of-speech (POS) trigrams to detect more fine-grained tendencies. Here, we again focus on the differences between female of higher class compared to the other groups. Relative entropy models are calculated on POS trigrams as described in Section 3.2.

Figure 3: Words contributing to differences between female of higher (FH) vs. lower class (FL) over time (color denotes relative frequency, size relative entropy, both relative to a time period)

The greatest difference in the use of POS trigrams lies between female of higher vs. lower class with an increasing tendency over time (see FHvsFL in Figure 4), while relative entropy is lower for FH vs. male production (MH and ML). This indicates that the distribution of POS trigrams of female higher class is more similar to both male of higher and lower class than female of lower class.

type	example	bits
Female lower class		
VP (interact.)	*I keep a (House)*	0.0039
VP (interact.)	*(I) keep the Hamtshire*	0.0030
CC	*but at last*	0.0027
CC	*and found all*	0.0025
VP (interact.)	*I would have*	0.0024
Female higher class		
VP (interact.; relat.)	*(I) am Nurse at*	0.0049
NP (gen.)	*his Wife's (Clothes)*	0.0035
VP (interact.; relat.)	*I am Wife (of)*	0.0027
VP (interact.; relat.)	*(I)* ***am the Wife*** *(of)*	0.0025
NP+	*(to my) House from Mr.*	0.0024

Table 2: Top 5 phrase/clause types for 1700

Inspecting which POS trigrams contribute to the difference between female of higher vs. lower

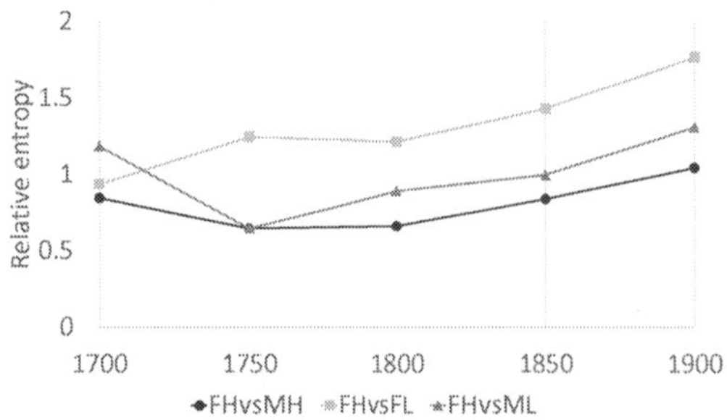

Figure 4: Relative entropy across fifty-years time periods in the OBC for females of higher class (FH) vs. male higher class (MH), female lower class (FL), and male lower class (ML)

type	example	bits
Female lower class		
VP (interact.)	*I had been*	0.0196
VP (interact.)	*asked me for*	0.0085
VP (interact.)	*said I was*	0.0080
VP (interact.)	*I could not*	0.0025
VP (interact.)	*me in the (face)*	0.0073
Female higher class		
NP+	***the intention of*** *committing*	0.0304
NP	*these are* ***the original invoices***	0.0208
VP (passive)	*my attention* ***was directed to***	0.0165
NP+	*contract* ***notes or cheques***	0.0161
VP (interact.)	***I was there*** *to attend*	0.0121

Table 3: Top 5 phrase/clause types for 1900

class, we consider the contribution in bits of each POS trigram. Table 2 and 3 show the top 5 POS trigrams categorized into phrase/clause types for 1700 and 1900, respectively. In 1700, FL are distinguished from FH by a pronounced interactional style, while FH from FL by an interactional style combined with relational clauses (see example (1)). Comparing the phrase/clause types diachronically, female of higher class develop over time a nominal style (see example (2)) that distinguishes them from female of lower class, who stick to an involved verbal style (VP interact.; see examples (3) and (4)). While this is in line with the observations made at the lexical level (cf. Section 4.1), we can see which phrase/clause types are used distinctively.

(1) *I am Nurse at the Hospital; Mr. Fern examin'd the Child; she has a soul Glect, and is ulcerated in the privy Parts.* (Female higher class 1733; HISCLASS 4; HISCO label: Professional Nurse, General)

(2) *I was taken to Bow Street, where a number of people were put up for the purposes of identification. [...] In fact, I picked somebody else, a man whom I afterwards discovered to be called George Dacey.* (Female higher class 1907; HISCLASS 4; HISCO label: Mail Distribution Clerk, General)

(3) *I keep a House in Bell-Yard in King's-street, Westminster, where I sell Greens and Fruit.* (Female lower class 1734; HISCLASS 11[6]; HISCO label: Other Street Vendors, Canvassers and News Vendors))

(4) *I am a barmaid at a public-house in Tottenham on April 10th I had been out, and as I was returning home I met the prosecutor he and I and another man walked along the road together [...]* (Female lower class 1902; HISCLASS 9; HISCO label: Bartender)

POS trigrams distinctive for female higher class against all other groups are shown in Table 4 for 1700 and Table 5 for 1900. In 1700 (Table 4), interactional style is a pronounced marker of distinction, with relational clauses when compared to FL (as shown in Table 2), and with adverbial phrases, possessive phrases and negation when compared to male production (MH and ML). Also, compared to either MH or ML, four out of five POS trigrams are identical (marked in bold). Thus, female higher class differ almost in the same way from male higher and lower class.

In 1900 (see Table 5), interactional style for FH is less distinctive (1 POS trigram compared to FL; 2 compared to MH; 1 compared to ML). Compared to FL, nominal style and passive voice are highest ranking. In comparison to both male productions (MH and ML), an adverbial/prepositional phrase and an interactional verb phrase are distinctive (marked in bold). In addition, compared to MH, a genitive noun phrase is highest ranking as well as a further adverbial phrase (AdvP). Comparison to both lower class groups (FL and ML) shows nominal style to be most distinctive: a noun phrase followed by a preposition (pointing to complex nominal phrases) is highest ranking (marked in bold).

To observe more general diachronic tendencies, we consider all top 30 POS trigrams of each comparison (i.e. for FHvsFL, FHvsMH and FHvsML). Based on the number of POS trigrams related to a

[6] 1-5 stand for higher, 6-13 for lower class.

comp.	type	POS trigram	example	bits	p-value
FHvsFL	VP (interact.) (relat.)	VB.NN1.IN	*(I) am Nurse at (the Hospital)*	0.00490	0.000107
	NP (gen.)	PP.NN1.GE	*his Wife's (Clothes)*	0.00345	0.033813
	VP (interact.) (relat.)	PPint.VB.NN1	*I am Wife (of Joseph Read)*	0.00270	0.008079
	VP (interact.) (relat.)	VB.DT.NN1	*(I) am the Wife (of Abraham Lacy)*	0.00247	0.002620
	NP+	NN1.IN.NN	*(to come to my) House from Mr. (Tull)*	0.00244	4.43E-05
FHvsMH	AdvP	**IN.PP.NN1**	*(I hid her) behind my Bed*	0.00435	0.000146
	VP (interact.) (adv.)	**PPint.VVD.RAloc**	*I came home (that Night about)*	0.00356	0.004452
	VP (interact.)	**PPint.VV0.DT**	*I keep a (Chandler's Shop)*	0.00246	0.006278
	VP (interact.)	CC.RR.PPint	*and so I (led her up stairs)*	0.00210	0.019882
	VP (interact.) (neg.)	**VV0.DT.NP**	*I can't (tell the Hour)*	0.00196	0.020611
FHvsML	AdvP	**IN.PP.NN1**	*(I hid her) behind my Bed*	0.00731	2.60E-06
	VP (interact.)	**PPint.VV0.DT**	*I keep a (Chandler's Shop)*	0.00526	8.03E-06
	VP (interact.) (neg.)	**VV0.DT.NP**	*I can't (tell the Hour)*	0.00349	0.002928
	VP (interact.) (poss.)	VVD.IN.PP	*(the Prisoner) came to my (House)*	0.00257	0.001892
	VP (interact.) (adv.)	**PPint.VVD.RAloc**	*I came home (that Night about)*	0.00185	0.042788

Table 4: Top 5 phrase/clause types for 1700 (overlapping POS trigrams across comparisons shown in bold)

comp.	type	POS trigram	example	bits	p-value
FHvsFL	NP+	**DT.NN1.INof**	*the intention of (committing suicide)*	0.03036	0.002835
	NP	DT.JJ.NN2	*(these are) the original invoices*	0.02075	0.028249
	VP (passive)	VBD.VVN.IN	*(my attention) was directed to (an advertisement)*	0.01649	0.035326
	NP+	NN2.CC.NN2	*(contract) notes or cheques*	0.01609	0.048210
	VP (interact.)	PPint.VBD.RAloc	*I was there (to attend)*	0.01211	0.046676
FHvsMH	AdvP/PrepP	**IN.PP.NN1**	*(this bill endorsed) by my husband*	0.01390	0.004174
	NP (gen.)	PP.NN1.GE	*my father's (banking account)*	0.00988	0.047651
	VP (interact.)	**PPint.VVD.PP**	*I saw him (sign a few letters)*	0.00887	0.020997
	AdvP	IN.DT.NPtemp	*(doing business) on a Sunday*	0.00614	0.046193
	VP (interact.)	CC.PPint.VVD	*and I made (no profit)*	0.00536	0.008897
FHvsML	NP+	**DT.NN1.INof**	*the intention of (committing suicide)*	0.01936	0.001253
	VP (interact.)	**PPint.VVD.PP**	*I saw him (sign a few letters)*	0.01069	0.002745
	NP+	NN1.INof.NN1	*(The) consignment of paper (came during)*	0.00830	0.020229
	AdvP/PrepP	**IN.PP.NN1**	*(this bill endorsed) by my husband*	0.00666	0.025071
	VP+	VVD.PP.IN	*(she) sent it to (me from Ostend)*	0.00365	0.015710

Table 5: Top 5 phrase/clause types for 1900 (overlapping POS trigrams across comparisons shown in bold)

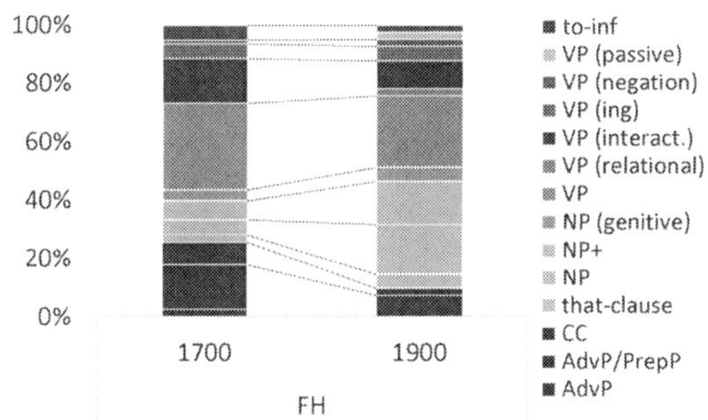

Figure 5: Percentage of top 30 POS trigrams by phrase/clause types distinctive for female of higher class (FH)

phrase type, we calculate the percentage of each phrase type distinctive of female higher class for both time periods (see Figure 5[7]). Red denotes phrase types which become less distinctive over time, yellow denotes phrase types more distinctive over time. While interactant verb phrases (VP interact.) become less distinctive for female higher class, nominal phrase types (NP genitive, NP+, NP) are considerably more distinctive over time. Phrases with conjunctions (CC; e.g. *he got up, and came to me*) as well as adverbial and prepositional phrases are less distinctive over time. The percentage of nominal style distinctive for female higher class increases over time (from 15% to 37%), while a distinctive verbal style decreases (from 56% to 49%), especially an interactant verbal style (from 15% to 9.8%) .

[7]From top to bottom: to-infinitives (to-inf), passive voice (VP passive), negation (VP negation), -ing form (VP ing) interactant verb phrases (VP interact.), simple verb phrase (VP), genitives (NP genitive), complex noun phrases (NP+, i.e. with prepositions or coordinative conjunctions), and simple noun phrases (NP), conjunctions (CC), adverbial and prepositional phrases (AdvP/PrepP), adverbial phrases of degree, location, comparison etc. based on the CLAWS7 tag set.

5 Conclusion

We have presented an approach to investigate stylistic variation across social variables and time at two linguistic levels: lexis and grammar. Our focus was on language use of female of higher class in court proceedings over the time span of approx. 200 years. We asked whether the uprising feminist movement from the mid-nineteenth century, questioning the women's inferior social position, is reflected in a change in language use of female higher class.

In terms of methods, we have used relative entropy according to Fankhauser et al. (2014), which allows us to measure the difference between probability distributions of linguistic units (here: words and POS trigrams). At the lexical level, lexical as well as stylistic differences have been identified. At the grammatical level, more fine-grained stylistic differences have been detected: female of higher class developed over time a nominal more informational style that increasingly differs from female of lower class.

While we have focused on female of higher class, in our ongoing work, we are analyzing the development of each group. Moreover, we will also consider the other roles in the trials, which will give more detailed insights into the development of language use in court trials. Also, while we use social class distinction based on higher and lower class, a more fine-grained distinction could be used as the OBC is annotated on a scale from 1-13. Instead of considering fifty-years time periods for comparison, in future work we aim to detect in which time span a particular change takes place.

In terms of contributions, by using an approach based on information theory (i.e. relative entropy), we are able to model language use and directly compare different groups of language users with one another, also obtaining linguistic units distinctively used across groups. The models are based on whole linguistic levels rather than on predefined features. This allows for a systematic account of language/stylistic variation. Also, we have shown that stylistic variation of groups may well change over time.

Acknowledgments

This research is funded by the German Research Foundation (Deutsche Forschungsgemeinschaft) under grants SFB1102: Information Density and Linguistic Encoding (www.sfb1102.uni-saarland.de) and the start-up grant for research projects from Saarland University. I would also like to thank the anonymous reviewers for their constructive and valuable comments, Peter Fankhauser (IDS Mannheim) for support in questions of data analysis, Stefan Fisher (Saarland University) for corpus processing, Magnus Huber (Giessen University) for questions on the OBC, and Elke Teich (Saarland University) for valuable comments on the first draft of this paper.

References

Ehsan Mohammady Ardehaly and Aron Culotta. 2015. Inferring Latent Attributes of Twitter Users with Label Regularization. In *Proceedings of the 2015 Conference of the North American Chapter of the Association for Computational Linguistics: Human Language Technologies*, pages 185–195, Denver, Colorado.

Shlomo Argamon, Moshe Koppel, James W. Pennebaker, and Jonathan Schler. 2007. Mining the Blogosphere: Age, Gender and the Varieties of Self-expression. *First Monday*, 12(9).

Federica Barbieri. 2008. Patterns of Age-based Linguistic Variation in American English. *Journal of Sociolinguistics*, 12(1):58–88.

Basil Bernstein. 1971. *Class, Code and Control: Volume 1 Theoretical Studies towards a Sociology of Language*. Routledge Taylor & Francis Group.

John D. Burger, John Henderson, George Kim, and Guido Zarrella. 2011. Discriminating Gender on Twitter. In *Proceedings of the 2011 Conference on Empirical Methods in Natural Language Processing*, pages 1301–1309, Edinburgh, Scotland, UK.

Susan Conrad and Douglas Biber. 2001. *Variation in English: Multi-Dimensional Studies*. Longman, London.

Cristian Danescu-Niculescu-Mizil, Moritz Sudhof, Dan Jurafsky, Jure Leskovec, and Christopher Potts. 2013. A Computational Approach to Politeness with Application to Social Factors. In *Proceedings of the 51st Annual Meeting of the Association for Computational Linguistics*, volume 1, pages 250–259, Sofia, Bulgaria. ALC.

Stefania Degaetano-Ortlieb, Hannah Kermes, Ashraf Khamis, and Elke Teich. to appear. *From Data to Evidence in English Language Research*, Language and Computers, chapter An Information-Theoretic Approach to Modeling Diachronic Change in Scientific English. Brill.

Stefania Degaetano-Ortlieb and Jannik Stroetgen. 2018. Diachronic Variation of Temporal Expressions in Scientific Writing Through the Lens of Relative Entropy. In *Language Technologies for the*

Challenges of the Digital Age: 27th International Conference, GSCL 2017, Berlin, Germany, September 13-14, 2017, Proceedings, volume 10713 of *Lecture Notes in Computer Science*, pages 259–275. Springer International Publishing.

Stefania Degaetano-Ortlieb and Elke Teich. 2016. Information-based Modeling of Diachronic Linguistic Change: From Typicality to Productivity. In *Proceedings of the 10th SIGHUM Workshop on Language Technology for Cultural Heritage, Social Sciences, and Humanities*, Berlin, Germany. ACL.

Stefania Degaetano-Ortlieb and Elke Teich. 2017. Modeling Intra-textual Variation with Entropy and Surprisal: Topical vs. Stylistic Patterns. In *Proceedings of the Joint LaTeCH and CLfL Workshop at ACL*, pages 68–77, Vancouver, Canada. ACL.

Penelope Eckert. 1989. *Social Categories and Identity in the High School*. Teachers College Press.

Penelope Eckert and Sally McConnell-Ginet. 2013. *Language and Gender*. Cambridge University Press, Cambridge.

Jacob Eisenstein. 2015. Written Dialect Variation in Online Social Media. In Charles Boberg, John Nerbonne, and Dom Watt, editors, *Handbook of Dialectology*. Wiley.

Jacob Eisenstein, Noah A. Smith, and Eric P. Xing. 2011. Discovering Sociolinguistic Associations with Structured Sparsity. In *Proceedings of the Association for Computational Linguistics (ACL)*, pages 1365–1374, Portland, OR.

Clive Emsley, Tim Hitchcock, and Robert Shoemaker. 2018. The Proceedings - The Value Of the Proceedings as a Historical Source. Old Bailey Proceedings Online, version 7.0.

Stefan Evert. 2005. *The CQP Query Language Tutorial*. IMS Stuttgart. CWB version 2.2.b90.

Peter Fankhauser, Jörg Knappen, and Elke Teich. 2014. Exploring and Visualizing Variation in Language Resources. In *Proceedings of the Ninth International Conference on Language Resources and Evaluation (LREC)*, Reykjavik, Iceland.

Lucie Flekova, Daniel Preotiuc-Pietro, and Lyle H. Ungar. 2016. Exploring Stylistic Variation with Age and Income on Twitter. In *Proceedings of the 54th Annual Meeting of the Association for Computational Linguistics*, pages 313–319, Berlin, Germany. ACL.

Dylan Glynn. 2014. Correspondence Analysis - Exploring Data and Identifying Patterns. In Dylan Glynn and Justyna A. Robinson, editors, *Corpus Methods for Semantics: Quantitative Studies in Polysemy and Synonymy*, volume 43 of *Human Cognitive Processing*, pages 443–485. John Benjamins, Amsterdam.

Mohammed Hasanuzzaman, Sabyasachi Kamila, Mandeep Kaur, Sriparna Saha, and Asif Ekbal. 2017. Temporal Orientation of Tweets for Predicting Income of Users. In *Proceedings of the 55th Annual Meeting of the Association for Computational Linguistics (Volume 2: Short Papers)*, pages 659–665. Association for Computational Linguistics.

Janet Holmes and Miriam Meyerhoff. 2003. *The Handbook of Language and Gender*. Wiley-Blackwell.

Dirk Hovy and Anders Søgaard. 2015. Tagging Performance Correlates with Author Age. In *Proceedings of the 53rd AnnualMeeting of the Association for Computational Linguistics and the 7th International Joint Conference on Natural Language Processing*, volume 2, pages 483–488, Beijing, China. ACL.

Magnus Huber, Magnus Nissel, and Karin Puga. 2016. *Old Bailey Corpus 2.0*. Hdl:11858/00-246C-0000-0023-8CFB-2.

Dan Jurafsky, Rajesh Ranganath, and Dan McFarland. 2009. Extracting Social Meaning: Identifying Interactional Style in Spoken Conversation. In *Proceedings of Human Language Technologies: The 2009 Annual Conference of the North American Chapter of the Association for Computational Linguistics*, pages 638–646, Boulder, Colorado.

Solomon Kullback and Richard A. Leibler. 1951. On Information and Sufficiency. *The Annals of Mathematical Statistics*, 22(1):79–86.

William Labov. 1963. The Social Motivation of a Sound Change. *Word*, 19(3):273–309.

James Milroy and Lesley Milroy. 1985. Linguistic Change, Social Network and Speaker Innovation. *Journal of Linguistics*, 21(2):339–384.

Lesley Milroy and Matthew Gordon. 2003. *Sociolinguistics: Method and Interpretation*. Wiley-Blackwell.

Dong Nguyen, A. Seza Dogruöz, Carolyn Penstein Rosé, and Franciska de Jong. 2016. Computational Sociolinguistics: A Survey. *CoRR*, abs/1508.07544.

Dong Nguyen, Dolf Trieschnigg, and Leonie Cornips. 2015. Audience and the Use of Minority Languages on Twitter. In *Proceedings of the Ninth International AAAI Conference on Web and Social Media*, pages 666–669, Oxford, UK.

Dong Nguyen, Dolf Trieschnigg, A. Seza Dogruöz, Rilana Gravel, Mariët Theune, Theo Meder, and Franciska de Jong. 2014. Why Gender and Age Prediction from Tweets is Hard: Lessons from a Crowdsourcing Experiment. In *Proceedings of COLING 2014, the 25th International Conference on Computational Linguistics: Technical Papers*, pages 1950–1961, Dublin, Ireland.

Claudia Peersman, Walter Daelemans, and Leona Van Vaerenbergh. 2011. Predicting Age and Gender in Online Social Networks. In *Proceedings of the 3rd International Workshop on Search and Mining User-generated Contents*, SMUC '11, pages 37–44, New York, NY, USA. ACM.

Vinodkumar Prabhakaran and Owen Rambow. 2017. Dialog Structure Through the Lens of Gender, Gender Environment, and Power. *Dialogue & Discourse*, 8(2):21–55.

Daniel Preoiuc-Pietro, Svitlana Volkova, Vasileios Lampos, Yoram Bachrach, and Nikolaos Aletras. 2015. Studying User Income through Language, Behaviour and Affect in Social Media. *PLOS ONE*, 10(9):1–17.

Daniel Preotiuc-Pietro, Vasileios Lampos, and Nikolaos Aletras. 2015a. An Analysis of the User Occupational Class through Twitter Content. In *Proceedings of the 53th Annual Meeting of the Association for Computational Linguistics and the 7th International Joint Conference of Natural Language Processing*, pages 1754–1764, Beijing, China. ACL.

H. Andrew Schwartz, Johannes C. Eichstaedt, Margaret L. Kern, Lukasz Dziurzynski, Stephanie M. Ramones, Megha Agrawal, Achal Shah, Michal Kosinski, David Stillwell, Martin E. P. Seligman, and Lyle H. Ungar. 2013. Personality, Gender, and Age in the Language of Social Media: The Open-Vocabulary Approach. *PLOS ONE*, 8(9):1–16.

Luke Sloan, Jeffrey Morgan, Pete Burnap, and Matthew Williams. 2015. Who Tweets? Deriving the Demographic Characteristics of Age, Occupation and Social Class from Twitter User Meta-Data. *PLOS ONE*, 10(3):1–20.

Sali A. Tagliamonte. 2006. *Analysing Sociolinguistic Variation*. Cambridge University Press, Cambridge.

Elke Teich, Stefania Degaetano-Ortlieb, Peter Fankhauser, Hannah Kermes, and Ekaterina Lapshinova-Koltunski. 2016. The Linguistic Construal of Disciplinarity: A Data-mining Approach Using Register Features. *Journal of the Association for Information Science and Technology (JAIST)*, 67(7):1668–1678.

Peter Trudgill. 1974. *The Social Differentiation of English in Norwich*. Cambridge University Press, Cambridge.

Suzanne E. Wagner. 2012. Age Grading in Sociolinguistic Theory. *Language and Linguistics Compass*, 6(6):371–382.

Uriel Weinreich, William Labov, and Marvin I. Herzog. 1968. Empirical Foundations for a Theory of Language Change. In Winfred P. Lehmann and Yakov Malkiel, editors, *Directions for Historical Linguistics: A Symposium*, pages 95–188. University of Texas Press, Austin.

Chengxiang Zhai and John Lafferty. 2004. A Study of Smoothing Methods for Language Models Applied to Information Retrieval. *ACM Transactions on Information Systems*, 22(2):179–214.

Stylistic Variation in Social Media Part-of-Speech Tagging

Murali Raghu Babu Balusu and **Taha Merghani** and **Jacob Eisenstein**
School of Interactive Computing
Georgia Institute of Technology
Atlanta, GA, USA
{b.murali, tmerghani3, jacobe}@gatech.edu

Abstract

Social media features substantial stylistic variation, raising new challenges for syntactic analysis of online writing. However, this variation is often aligned with author attributes such as age, gender, and geography, as well as more readily-available social network metadata. In this paper, we report new evidence on the link between language and social networks in the task of part-of-speech tagging. We find that tagger error rates are correlated with network structure, with high accuracy in some parts of the network, and lower accuracy elsewhere. As a result, tagger accuracy depends on training from a balanced sample of the network, rather than training on texts from a narrow subcommunity. We also describe our attempts to add robustness to stylistic variation, by building a mixture-of-experts model in which each expert is associated with a region of the social network. While prior work found that similar approaches yield performance improvements in sentiment analysis and entity linking, we were unable to obtain performance improvements in part-of-speech tagging, despite strong evidence for the link between part-of-speech error rates and social network structure.

1 Introduction

Social media feature greater diversity than the formal genres that constitute classic datasets such as the Penn Treebank (Marcus et al., 1993) and the Brown Corpus (Francis and Kucera, 1982): there are more authors, more *kinds* of authors, more varied communicative settings, fewer rules, and more stylistic variation (Baldwin et al., 2013; Eisenstein, 2013). Previous work has demonstrated precipitous declines in the performance of state-of-the-art systems for core tasks such as part-of-speech tagging (Gimpel et al., 2011) and named-entity recognition (Ritter et al., 2010) when these systems are applied to social media text, and stylistic diversity seems the likely culprit. However, we still lack quantitative evidence of the role played by language variation in the performance of NLP systems in social media, and existing solutions to this problem are piecemeal at best. In this paper, we attempt to address both issues: we quantify the impact of one form of sociolinguistic variation on part-of-speech tagging accuracy, and we design a model that attempts to adapt to this variation.

Our contribution focuses on the impact of language variation that is aligned with one or more *social networks* among authors on the microblogging platform Twitter. We choose Twitter because language styles in this platform are particularly diverse (Eisenstein et al., 2010), and because moderately large labeled datasets are available (Gimpel et al., 2011; Owoputi et al., 2013). We choose social networks for several reasons. First, they can readily be obtained from both metadata and behavioral traces on multiple social media platforms (Huberman et al., 2008). Second, social networks are strongly correlated with "demographic" author-level variables such as age (Rosenthal and McKeown, 2011), gender (Eckert and McConnell-Ginet, 2003), race (Green, 2002), and geography (Trudgill, 1974), thanks to the phenomenon of *homophily*, also known as *assortative mixing* (McPherson et al., 2001; Al Zamal et al., 2012). These demographic variables are in turn closely linked to language variation in American English (Wolfram and Schilling-Estes, 2005), and have been shown to improve some document classification tasks (Hovy, 2015). Third, there is growing evidence of the strong relationship between social network structures and language variation, even beyond the extent to which the social network acts as a proxy for demographic attributes (Milroy, 1991; Dodsworth, 2017).

Proceedings of the 2nd Workshop on Stylistic Variation, pages 11–19
New Orleans, Louisiana, June 5, 2018.

To measure the impact of socially-linked language variation, we focus on part-of-speech tagging, a fundamental task for syntactic analysis. First, we measure the extent to which tagger performance is correlated with network structure, finding that tagger performance on friends is significantly more correlated than would be expected by chance. We then design alternative training and test splits that are aligned with network structure, and find that test set performance decreases in this scenario, which corresponds to domain adaptation across social network communities. This speaks to the importance of covering all relevant social network communities in training data.

We then consider how to address the problem of language variation, by building social awareness into a recurrent neural tagging model. Our modeling approach is inspired by Yang and Eisenstein (2017), who train a mixture-of-experts for sentiment analysis, where the expert weights are computed from social network node embeddings. But while prior work demonstrated improvements in sentiment analysis and information extraction (Yang et al., 2016), this approach does not yield any gains on part-of-speech tagging. We conclude the paper by briefly considering possible reasons for this discrepancy, and propose approaches for future work in social adaptation of syntactic analysis.[1]

2 Data

We use the corrected[2] OCT27 dataset from Gimpel et al. (2011) and Owoputi et al. (2013) as our training set, which contains part-of-speech annotations for 1,827 tweets sampled from Oct 27-28, 2010. We use the train and dev splits of OCT27 as our training dataset and the test split of OCT27 dataset as our validation dataset. The DAILY547 dataset from Owoputi et al. (2013) which has 547 tweets is used for evaluation. Table 2 specifies the number of tweets and tokens in each dataset. The tagset for this dataset is explained in Owoputi et al. (2013); it differs significantly from the Penn Treebank and Universal Dependencies tagsets.

In September 2017, we extracted author IDs for each of the tweets and constructed three author social networks based on the follow, mention, and retweet relations between the authors in the dataset, which we refer to as *follow*, *mention* and *retweet* networks in Table 2. Specifically, we use the Twitter API to crawl the friends of the OCT27 and DAILY547 users (individuals that they follow) and the most recent 3,200 tweets in their timelines. The mention and retweet links are then extracted from the tweet text and metadata. Table 2 specifies the total number of authors (whose tweets exist in our dataset) in each network, the total number of nodes and the total number of relations among these nodes. We treat all social networks as undirected graphs, where two users are socially connected if there exists at least one social relation between them. Several authors of the tweets can no longer be queried from Twitter, possibly because their accounts have been deleted. They are not included in the network, but their tweets are still used for training and evaluation.

Dataset	#Msg.	#Tok.
OCT27	1,827	26,594
DAILY547	547	7,707

Table 1: Annotated datasets: number of messages and tokens

Network	#Authors	#Nodes	#Edges
Follow	1,280	905,751	1,239,358
Mention	1,217	384,190	623,754
Retweet	1,154	182,390	314,381

Table 2: Statistics for each social network

3 Linguistic Homophily

The hypothesis of *linguistic homophily* is that socially connected individuals tend to use language similarly, as compared to randomly selected pairs of individuals who are not socially connected (Yang and Eisenstein, 2017). We now describe two pilot studies that test this hypothesis.

3.1 Assortativity

We test whether errors in POS tagging are *assortative* on the social networks defined in the previous section: that is, if two individuals (i, j) are connected in the network, then a model's error on the tweets of author i suggests that the errors on the tweets of author j are more likely. To measure assortativity, we compute the average difference in the tagger's per-token accuracy on tweets for au-

[1] Code for rerunning the experiments is available here: https://github.com/bmurali1994/socialnets_postagging

[2] Owoputi et al. corrected inconsistencies in the ground labeling of *that/this* in 100 (about 0.4%) total labels.

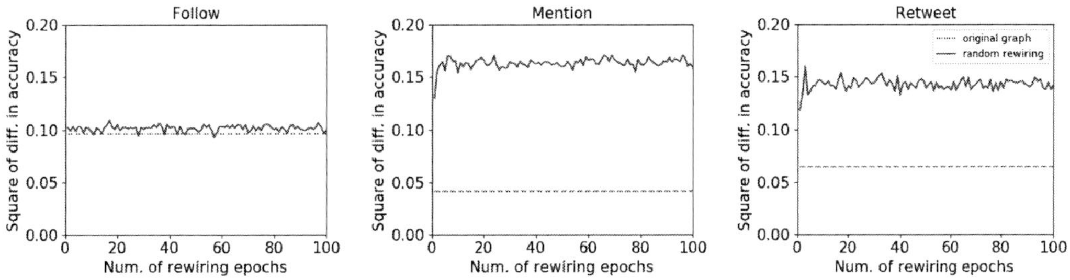

(a) Most-common-tag baseline tagger

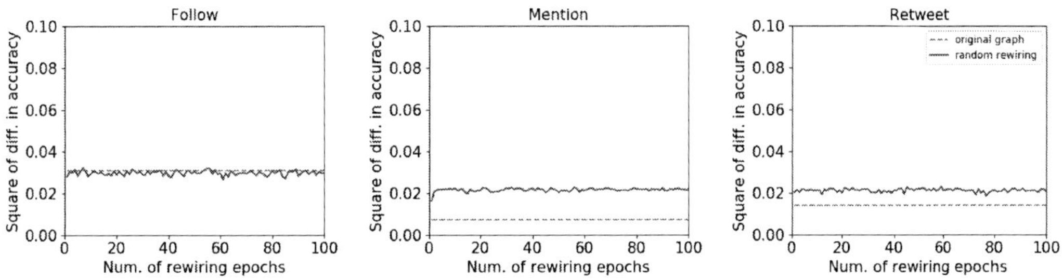

(b) Pre-trained MEMM tagger from Owoputi et al. (2013).

Figure 1: Average of the squared difference in tagging accuracy on observed (red) and randomized networks (blue).

thors i and j, averaged over all connected pairs in the network. This measures whether classification errors are related on the network structure.

We compare the observed assortativity against the assortativity in a network that has been randomly rewired. Each rewiring epoch involves a number of random rewiring operations equal to the total number of edges in the network. The edges are randomly selected, so a given edge may not be rewired in each epoch; furthermore, the degree of each node is preserved throughout. If the squared difference in accuracy is lower for the observed networks than for their rewired counterparts, this would indicate that tagger accuracy is correlated with network structure. Figure 2 explains the metric and rewiring briefly through an example.

We compute the assortativity for three taggers:

- We first use a naïve tagger, which predicts the most common tag seen during training if the word exists in the vocabulary, and otherwise predicts the the most common tag for an unseen word. Preprocessing of each tweet involves lowercasing, normalizing all @-mentions to $\langle @MENTION \rangle$, and normalizing URLs and email addresses to a common token (e.g. $http : //bit.ly/dP8rR8 \Rightarrow \langle URL \rangle$).

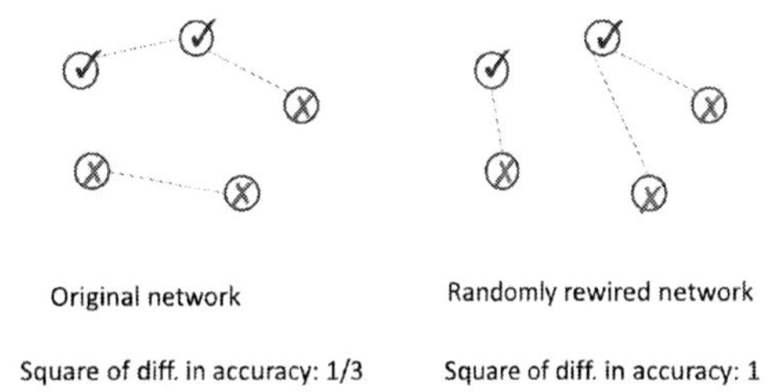

Figure 2: Toy example: differences in tagging accuracy on original and randomly-rewired network.

- We train a lexical, feature-rich CRF model. Lexical features in the CRF model include the word, previous two words, next two words, prefixes and suffixes of the previous two, current and next two words, and flags for special characters like hyphen, at-mention, hashtag, hyphen and digits in the current word.

- Finally, we repeat these experiments with the pretrained maximum entropy Markov model (MEMM) tagger from (Owoputi et al., 2013), trained on OCT27 tweets.

Figure 1 shows the results for the naïve tagger and the MEMM tagger; the results were similar for the CRF were similar. Tagger accuracy is well correlated with network structure in the mention and retweet graphs, consistent with the hypothesis of linguistic homophily. These findings support prior work suggesting that "behavioral" social networks such as mentions and retweets are more meaningful than "articulated" networks like the follower graph (Huberman et al., 2008; Puniyani et al., 2010).

3.2 Clustering

Next, we examine whether linguistic homophily can lead to mismatches between the test and training data. We embed each author's social network position into a vector representation of dimension D_v, using the LINE method for social network node embedding (Tang et al., 2015). These embeddings are obtained solely from the social network, and not from the text.

We obtain $D_v = 50$-dimensional node embeddings, and apply k-means clustering (Hartigan and Wong, 1979) to obtain two sets of authors (train and test). By design, the training and test sets will be in different regions of the network, so training and test authors will be unlikely to be socially connected. We then train the lexical CRF tagger on the training set, and apply it to the test set. The same setup is then applied to a randomly-selected training/test split, in which the social network structure is ignored. This comparison is illustrated in Figure 3. We repeat this experiment for 10 times for all three social networks: follow, mention and retweet.

The theory of linguistic homophily implies that the test set performance should be *worse* in the case that the test set and training sets are drawn from different parts of the network, since the linguistic style in the training set will not match the test data. In contrast, when the training and test sets are drawn in a manner that is agnostic to network structure, the training and test sets are expected to be more linguistically similar, and therefore, test set performance should be better. As shown in Table 3, the results support the theory: predictive accuracy is higher when the test and training sets are not drawn from different parts of the network.

Network	Network clusters	Random
Follow	82.01%	83.83%
Mention	81.40%	83.07%
Retweet	81.01%	83.52%

Table 3: Comparison of tagger accuracy using network-based and random training/test splits

4 Adapting to socially-linked variation

In this section, we describe a neural network method that leverages social network information to improve part-of-speech tagging. We employ the *Social Attention* neural network architecture, where the system prediction is the weighted combination of the outputs of several basis models (Yang and Eisenstein, 2017). We encourage each basis model to focus on a local region of the social network, so that classification on socially connected individuals employs similar model combinations. This allows sharing of strength for some similar properties between these network components.

In this architecture, each prediction is the weighted combination of the outputs of several basis models. Given a set of labeled instances $\{\boldsymbol{x}_i, \boldsymbol{y}_i\}$ and authors $\{a_i\}$, the goal of personalized probabilistic classification is to estimate a conditional label distribution $p(\boldsymbol{y} \mid \boldsymbol{x}, a)$. We condition on the author a by modeling the conditional label distribution as a mixture over the posterior distributions of K basis taggers,

$$p(\boldsymbol{y} \mid \boldsymbol{x}, a) = \sum_{k=1}^{K} \pi_{a,k} \times p_k(\boldsymbol{y} \mid \boldsymbol{x}) \quad (1)$$

The basis taggers $p_k(\boldsymbol{y} \mid \boldsymbol{x})$ can be arbitrary conditional distributions. We use a hierarchical recurrent neural network model, in addition to a tag dictionary and Brown cluster surface features (Brown et al., 1992), which we describe in more detail in § 4.2. The component weighting distribution $\pi_{a,k}$ is conditioned on the social network G, and functions as an attentional mechanism, described in § 4.1. The main idea is that for a pair of authors a_i and a_j who are nearby in the social network G, the prediction rules should behave similarly if the attentional distributions are similar, i.e., $\pi_{a_i,k} \approx \pi_{a_j,k}$. If we have labeled training data for a_i and wish to make predictions on author a_j, some of the personalization from a_i will be shared by a_j. The overall classification approach can be viewed as a mixture of experts (Jacobs et al., 1991), leveraging the social network

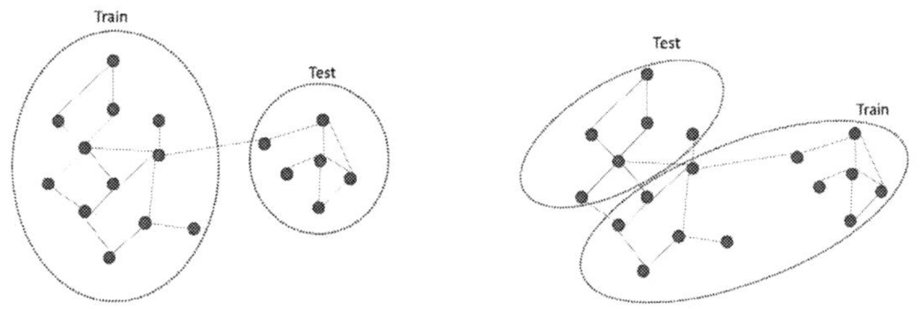

Figure 3: (left) Network-aligned train/test split and (right) random train/test split

as side information to choose the distribution over experts for each author.

4.1 Social Attention Model

The goal of the social attention model is to assign similar basis weights to authors who are nearby in the social network G. We operationalize social proximity by embedding each author's social network position into a vector representation, again using the LINE method for node embedding (Tang et al., 2015). The resulting embeddings v_a are treated as fixed parameters in a probabilistic model over edges in the social network. These embeddings are learned solely from the social network G, without leveraging any textual information. The attentional weights are then computed from the embeddings using a softmax layer,

$$\pi_{a,k} = \frac{\exp(\boldsymbol{\phi}_k \cdot \boldsymbol{v}_a + b_k)}{\sum_{k'}^{K} \exp(\boldsymbol{\phi}_{k'} \cdot \boldsymbol{v}_a + b_{k'})}. \quad (2)$$

The parameters $\boldsymbol{\phi}_k$ and b_k are learned in the model. We observed that almost 50% of the authors in our dataset do not appear in any social network. For all these authors, we use the same embedding $\boldsymbol{v}'$ to let the model learn the proportion weight of the individual basis models in the ensemble. This embedding $\boldsymbol{v}'$ is also learned as a parameter in the model. We have also tried computing the attentional weights using a sigmoid function,

$$\pi_{a,k} = \sigma(\boldsymbol{\phi}_k \cdot \boldsymbol{v}_a + b_k), \quad (3)$$

so that $\boldsymbol{\pi}_a$ is not normalized, but the results were quite similar.

4.2 Modeling Surface Features

We use surface-level features in addition to the basis models to improve the performance of our model closer to the state-of-the-art results. Specifically, we use the tag dictionary features and the Brown cluster features as described by Gimpel et al. (2011).

Since Brown clusters are hierarchical in a binary tree, each word is associated with a tree path represented as a bitstring with length ≤ 16; we use prefixes of the bitstring as features (for all prefix lengths $\in \{2, 4, 6, ..., 16\}$). Concatenating the Brown cluster features of the previous and next token along with the current token helped improve the performance of the baseline model.

We also used the tag dictionary features from Gimpel et al. (2011), by adding features for a word's most frequent part-of-speech tags from Penn Treebank and Universal Dependencies. This also helped improve the performance of the baseline model. We found these surface features to be vital. Nonetheless, we were not able to match the performance of the state-of-the-art systems.

4.3 POS tagging with Hierarchical LSTMs

We next describe the baseline model: $p_k(\boldsymbol{y} \mid \boldsymbol{x})$. The baseline model is a word-level bi-LSTM, with a character-level bi-LSTM to compute the embeddings of the words (Ling et al., 2015). In addition to the embeddings from the character level bi-LSTM, we also learn the word embeddings which are initialized randomly and also use fixed pretrained GloVe Twitter (Pennington et al., 2014) embeddings for the word-level bi-LSTM. The final input to the word-level LSTM is the concatenation of the embedding from the character level, learned word embedding and the fixed pretrained word embedding. The final hidden state for each word $\boldsymbol{h}_i$ is obtained and concatenated with the surface features for each word $\boldsymbol{s}_i^k$, and the result is passed through a fully connected neural network, giving a latent representation $\boldsymbol{r}_i^k$. The conditional probability is then computed as,

$$p_k(y_i = t \mid x_i) = \frac{\exp(\boldsymbol{\beta}_t \cdot \boldsymbol{r}_i^k + c_t)}{\sum_{t'} \exp(\boldsymbol{\beta}_{t'} \cdot \boldsymbol{r}_i^k + c_{t'})}. \quad (4)$$

4.4 Loss Function and Training

We train the ensemble model by minimizing the negative log likelihood of the tags for all the tokens in all the tweets in the training dataset.

Alternative objectives We have also tried training the model using a hinge loss, but the results were similar and hence excluded in the paper. We also explored a variational autoencoder (VAE) framework (Kingma and Welling, 2014), in which the node embeddings were modeled with a latent vector z, which was used both to control the mixture weights π_k, and to reconstruct the node embeddings. Again, results were similar to those obtained with the simpler negative log-likelihood objective.

Training problems One potential problem with this framework is that after initialization, a small number of basis models may claim most of the mixture weights for all the users, while other basis models are inactive. This can occur because some basis models may be initialized with parameters that are globally superior. As a result, the "dead" basis models will receive near-zero gradient updates, and therefore can never improve. Careful initialization of the parameters ϕ_k and b_k and using L2-regularization parameters of the model helped mitigate the issue to some extent. Using the attentional weights computed using the sigmoid function as described in Equation 3 does not have this problem, but the final evaluation results were quite similar to the model with attentional weights computed using softmax as mentioned in Equation 2.

5 Experiments

Our evaluation focuses on the DAILY547 dataset (Owoputi et al., 2013). We train our system on the train and dev splits of the OCT27 dataset (Gimpel et al., 2011) and use the test split of OCT27 as our validation dataset and evaluate on the DAILY547 dataset. Accuracy of the tokens is our evaluation metric for the model. We compare our results to our baseline model and the state of the art results on the Twitter OCT27+Daily547 dataset.

5.1 Experimental Settings

We use 100-dimensional pretrained Twitter GloVe embeddings (Pennington et al., 2014) which are trained on about two billion tweets. We use one-layer for both the character-level and the word-level bi-LSTM model with hidden state sizes of 50 and 150 dimensions respectively. The dimensions of character embeddings is set to be 30 and the learned word embeddings is 50. We use tanh activation functions all throughout the model and use Xavier initialization (Glorot and Bengio, 2010) for the parameters. The model is trained with ADAM optimizer (Kingma and Ba, 2014) on L2-regularized negative log-likelihood. The regularization strength was set to 0.01, and the dropout was set to 0.35. The best hyper-parameters for the number of basis classifiers is $K = 3$ for the follow and mention networks, and $K = 4$ for the retweet network.

System	Accuracy
Owoputi et. al.	**92.80%**
BiLSTM tagger	90.50%
Ensemble of BiLSTM taggers	90.11%
BiLSTM taggers with social attention	89.80%

Table 4: Accuracy of the models on the DAILY547 dataset. The best results are in **bold**.

Network	Accuracy
Follow	89.42%
Mention	89.80%
Retweet	89.65%

Table 5: Accuracy of the social attention model, across each of the three networks.

5.2 Results and Discussion

Table 4 summarizes the main empirical findings, where we report results from author embeddings trained on the mention network for Social Attention. The results of different social networks with Social Attention is shown in Table 5.

We also evaluate the performance of the trained Social Attention model on the subset of authors who can be located in the social network. The accuracy on these authors is similar to the overall performance on the full dataset. We also observe the attention distributions of the authors in the social network on the basis models in the ensemble. For every pair of authors a_i and a_j connected in the social network we compute $\Sigma_k|\pi_{a_i,k} - \pi_{a_j,k}|$ and average it across all pairs in the network. This

Network	Actual Network	Random
Follow	0.90	1.10
Mention	0.38	1.06
Retweet	0.36	0.68

Table 6: Comparison of the mean absolute difference in attention distributions of connected authors in actual social networks versus randomly rewired networks.

is compared with against a randomly rewired network. If this value is lower for the social network, then this indicates that the connected authors tend to have similar attentional distributions as explained in § 4. The results are presented in Table 6. These results clearly indicate that the authors who are connected in the social network tend to have similar attentional distributions.

While the analyses in § 3 indicated a strong degree of linguistic homophily, we do not observe any significant gain in performance. We think the following factors played an important role:

Missing authors. There are a large number of missing authors in each of the social network (about 50% of the authors of the tweets in the dataset). The results from combining all the three social networks by just concatenating this embeddings did not help either in our experiments.

Tweets per author. We have only one tweet for every author in our dataset and this makes it harder for the model to extract relations between authors and their tweets.

Dataset size. The dataset contains only 2374 tweets, which could be the reason our deep learning model is still behind the feature-rich Markov Model of Owoputi et al. (2013) by about 2%.

Sparse social networks. The social networks that we constructed using the twitter IDs from the tweet metadata of the OCT27 and DAILY547 datasets were very sparse, and the node degree distributions (number of edges per node) have high variance.

6 Related Work

Previous problems on incorporating social relations have focused on sentiment analysis and entity linking, where the existence of social relations between users is considered as a clue that the sentiment polarities in the messages from the users should be similar or the entities that they refer to in their messages are the same. Speriosu et al. (2011) constructs a heterogeneous network with tweets, users, and n-grams as nodes, and the sentiment label distributions associated with the nodes are refined by performing label propagation over social relations. Tan et al. (2011) and Hu et al. (2013) leverage social relations for sentiment analysis by exploiting a factor graph model and the graph Laplacian technique respectively, so that the tweets belonging to social connected users share similar label distributions. Yang et al. (2016) proposed a neural based structured learning architecture for tweet entity linking, leveraging the tendency of socially linked individuals to share similar interests on named entities — the phenomenon of entity homophily. Yang and Eisenstein (2017) proposed a middle ground between group-level demographic characteristics and personalization, by exploiting social network structure. We extend this work by applying it for the first time to syntactic analysis.

7 Conclusion

This paper describes the hypothesis of linguistic homophily specifically linked to stylistic variation on social media data and tests the effectiveness of social attention to overcome language variation, leveraging the tendency of socially proximate individuals to use language similarly for POS tagging. While our preliminary analyses demonstrate a strong correlation between tagging accuracy and network structure, we are unable to leverage these correlations for improvements in tagging accuracy.

How should we reconcile these conflicting results? In the limit of infinite resources, we could train separate taggers for separate treebanks, featuring each language variety. But even if language variation is strongly associated with the network structure, the effectiveness of this approach would still be limited by the inherent difficulty of tagging each language variety. In other words, augmenting the tagger with social network metadata may not help much, because some parts of the network may simply be harder to tag than others. However, this pessimistic conclusion must be offset by noting the small size of existing annotated datasets for social media writing, which are orders of magnitude smaller than comparable corpora of newstext. While some online varieties maybe hard to tag well, it is equally possible that the advantages of more flexible modeling frameworks only become visible when there is sufficient data to accurately estimate them. We are particularly interested to explore the utility of semi-supervised techniques for training such models in future work.

References

Faiyaz Al Zamal, Wendy Liu, and Derek Ruths. 2012. Homophily and latent attribute inference: Inferring latent attributes of Twitter users from neighbors. In *Proceedings of the International Conference on Web and Social Media (ICWSM)*. pages 387–390.

Timothy Baldwin, Paul Cook, Marco Lui, Andrew MacKinlay, and Li Wang. 2013. How noisy social media text, how diffrnt social media sources. In *Proceedings of the 6th International Joint Conference on Natural Language Processing (IJCNLP 2013)*. pages 356–364.

Peter F Brown, Peter V Desouza, Robert L Mercer, Vincent J Della Pietra, and Jenifer C Lai. 1992. Class-based n-gram models of natural language. *Computational linguistics* 18(4):467–479.

Robin Dodsworth. 2017. Migration and dialect contact. *Annual Review of Linguistics* 3(1):331–346.

P. Eckert and S. McConnell-Ginet. 2003. *Language and Gender*. Cambridge Textbooks in Linguistics. Cambridge University Press.

Jacob Eisenstein. 2013. What to do about bad language on the internet. In *Proceedings of the North American Chapter of the Association for Computational Linguistics (NAACL)*. pages 359–369.

Jacob Eisenstein, Brendan O'Connor, Noah A. Smith, and Eric P. Xing. 2010. A latent variable model for geographic lexical variation. In *Proceedings of Empirical Methods for Natural Language Processing (EMNLP)*. pages 1277–1287.

W Francis and Henry Kucera. 1982. *Frequency analysis of English usage*. Houghton Mifflin Company.

Kevin Gimpel, Nathan Schneider, Brendan O'Connor, Dipanjan Das, Daniel Mills, Jacob Eisenstein, Michael Heilman, Dani Yogatama, Jeffrey Flanigan, and Noah A Smith. 2011. Part-of-speech tagging for twitter: Annotation, features, and experiments. *ACL* pages 42–47.

Xavier Glorot and Yoshua Bengio. 2010. Understanding the difficulty of training deep feedforward neural networks. In Yee Whye Teh and Mike Titterington, editors, *Proceedings of the Thirteenth International Conference on Artificial Intelligence and Statistics*. PMLR, Chia Laguna Resort, Sardinia, Italy, volume 9 of *Proceedings of Machine Learning Research*, pages 249–256.

L.J. Green. 2002. *African American English: A Linguistic Introduction*. Cambridge University Press.

J. A. Hartigan and M. A. Wong. 1979. A k-means clustering algorithm. *JSTOR: Applied Statistics* 28(1):100–108.

Dirk Hovy. 2015. Demographic factors improve classification performance. *ACL* pages 752–762.

Xia Hu, Lei Tang, Jiliang Tang, and Huan Liu. 2013. Exploiting social relations for sentiment analysis in microblogging. In *Proceedings of the Sixth ACM International Conference on Web Search and Data Mining*. ACM, New York, NY, USA, WSDM '13, pages 537–546.

Bernardo A. Huberman, Daniel M. Romero, and Fang Wu. 2008. Social networks that matter: Twitter under the microscope. *CoRR* abs/0812.1045.

Robert A. Jacobs, Michael I. Jordan, Steven J. Nowlan, and Geoffrey E. Hinton. 1991. Adaptive mixtures of local experts. *Neural Comput.* 3(1):79–87.

Diederik P. Kingma and Jimmy Ba. 2014. Adam: A method for stochastic optimization. *CoRR* abs/1412.6980.

Diederik P Kingma and Max Welling. 2014. Auto-encoding variational bayes. In *Proceedings of the International Conference on Learning Representations (ICLR)*.

Wang Ling, Chris Dyer, Alan W Black, Isabel Trancoso, Ramon Fermandez, Silvio Amir, Luis Marujo, and Tiago Luis. 2015. Finding function in form: Compositional character models for open vocabulary word representation. *Proceedings of Empirical Methods for Natural Language Processing (EMNLP)* pages 1520–1530.

Mitchell P. Marcus, Mary Ann Marcinkiewicz, and Beatrice Santorini. 1993. Building a large annotated corpus of English: The Penn Treebank. *Computational Linguistics* 19(2):313–330.

Miller McPherson, Lynn Smith-Lovin, and James M Cook. 2001. Birds of a feather: Homophily in social networks. *Annual review of sociology* 27(1):415–444.

Lesley Milroy. 1991. *Language and Social Networks*. Wiley-Blackwell, 2 edition.

Olutobi Owoputi, Brendan O'Connor, Chris Dyer, Kevin Gimpel, Nathan Schneider, and Noah A Smith. 2013. Improved part-of-speech tagging for online conversational text with word clusters. *Proceedings of North American Association for Computational Linguistics (NAACL)* .

Jeffrey Pennington, Richard Socher, and Christopher D. Manning. 2014. Glove: Global vectors for word representation. In *Proceedings of Empirical Methods for Natural Language Processing (EMNLP)*. pages 1532–1543.

Kriti Puniyani, Jacob Eisenstein, Shay Cohen, and Eric P. Xing. 2010. Social links from latent topics in microblogs. In *Proceedings of NAACL Workshop on Social Media*. Los Angeles.

Alan Ritter, Colin Cherry, and Bill Dolan. 2010. Unsupervised modeling of twitter conversations. In *Human Language Technologies: The 2010 Annual Conference of the North American Chapter of the Association for Computational Linguistics*. Association for Computational Linguistics, Stroudsburg, PA, USA, HLT '10, pages 172–180.

Sara Rosenthal and Kathleen McKeown. 2011. Age prediction in blogs: A study of style, content, and online behavior in pre-and post-social media generations. In *Proceedings of the 49th Annual Meeting of the Association for Computational Linguistics: Human Language Technologies-Volume 1*. Association for Computational Linguistics, pages 763–772.

Michael Speriosu, Nikita Sudan, Sid Upadhyay, and Jason Baldridge. 2011. Twitter polarity classification with label propagation over lexical links and the follower graph. In *Proceedings of the First Workshop on Unsupervised Learning in NLP*. Association for Computational Linguistics, Stroudsburg, PA, USA, EMNLP '11, pages 53–63.

Chenhao Tan, Lillian Lee, Jie Tang, Long Jiang, Ming Zhou, and Ping Li. 2011. User-level sentiment analysis incorporating social networks. In *Proceedings of the 17th ACM SIGKDD International Conference on Knowledge Discovery and Data Mining*. ACM, New York, NY, USA, KDD '11, pages 1397–1405.

Jian Tang, Meng Qu, Mingzhe Wang, Ming Zhang, Jun Yan, and Qiaozhu Mei. 2015. Line: Large-scale information network embedding. In *WWW*. ACM.

Peter Trudgill. 1974. Linguistic change and diffusion: description and explanation in sociolinguistic dialect geography. *Language in Society* 3(2):215246.

Walt Wolfram and Natalie Schilling-Estes. 2005. *American English: dialects and variation*. Wiley-Blackwell, second edition.

Yi Yang, Ming-Wei Chang, and Jacob Eisenstein. 2016. Toward socially-infused information extraction: Embedding authors, mentions, and entities. In *Proceedings of Empirical Methods for Natural Language Processing (EMNLP)*.

Yi Yang and Jacob Eisenstein. 2017. Overcoming language variation in sentiment analysis with social attention. *Transactions of the Association for Computational Linguistics (TACL)* 5.

Detecting Syntactic Features of Translated Chinese

Hai Hu, Wen Li, Sandra Kübler
Indiana University
{huhai,wl9,skuebler}@indiana.edu

Abstract

We present a machine learning approach to distinguish texts translated to Chinese (by humans) from texts originally written in Chinese, with a focus on a wide range of syntactic features. Using Support Vector Machines (SVMs) as classifier on a genre-balanced corpus in translation studies of Chinese, we find that constituent parse trees and dependency triples as features without lexical information perform very well on the task, with an F-measure above 90%, close to the results of lexical n-gram features, without the risk of learning topic information rather than translation features. Thus, we claim syntactic features alone can accurately distinguish translated from original Chinese. Translated Chinese exhibits an increased use of determiners, subject position pronouns, NP + "的" as NP modifiers, multiple NPs or VPs conjoined by "、", among other structures. We also interpret the syntactic features with reference to previous translation studies in Chinese, particularly the usage of pronouns.

1 Introduction

Work in translation studies has shown that translated texts differ significantly in subtle and not so subtle ways from original, non-translated texts. For example, Volansky et al. (2013) show that the prefix *mono-* is more frequent in Greek-to-English translations because epistemologically it originates from Greek. Also, the structure of modal verb, infinitive, and past participle (e.g. *must be taken*) is more prevalent in translated English from 10 source languages.

We also know that a machine learning based approach can distinguish translated from original texts with high accuracy for Indo-European languages such as Italian (Baroni and Bernardini, 2005), Spanish (Ilisei et al., 2010), and English (Volansky et al., 2013; Lembersky et al., 2012; Koppel and Ordan, 2011). Features used in those studies include common bag-of-words features, such as word n-grams, as well as part-of-speech (POS) n-grams, function words, etc. Although such surface features yield very high accuracy (in the high nineties), they do not contain much deeper syntactic information, which is key in interpreting textual styles. Furthermore, despite the large amount of research on Indo-European languages, few studies have quantitatively investigated either lexical or syntactic features of translated Chinese, and to our knowledge, no automatic classification experiments have been conducted for this language.

Thus the purpose of this paper is two-fold: First, we perform translated vs. original text classification on a balanced corpus of Chinese, in order to verify whether translationese in Chinese is as real as it is in Indo-European languages, and to discover which structures are prominent in translated but not original Chinese texts. Second, we show that using only syntactic features without any lexical information, such as context-free grammar (CFG), subtrees of constituent parses, and dependency triples, perform almost as well as lexical n-gram features, confirming the translationese hypothesis from a purely syntactic point of view. These features are also easily interpretable for linguists interested in syntactic styles of translated Chinese. We analyze the top syntactic features ranked by a common feature selection algorithm, and interpret them with reference to previous studies on translationese features in Chinese.

2 Related Work

2.1 Translated vs. Original Classification

The pioneering work of Baroni and Bernardini (2005) is one of the first to use machine learning methods to distinguish translated and orig-

Proceedings of the 2nd Workshop on Stylistic Variation, pages 20–28
New Orleans, Louisiana, June 5, 2018.

inal (Italian) texts. They experimented with word/lemma/POS n-grams and mixed representations and reached an F-measure of 86% using recall maximizing combinations of SVM classifiers. In the mixed n-gram representation, they used inflected wordforms for function words, but replaced content words with their POS tags. The high F-measure (85.2%) with such features shows that "function word distributions and shallow syntactic patterns" without any lexical information can already account for much of the characteristics of translated text.

Volansky et al. (2013) is a very comprehensive study that investigated translationese in English by looking at original and translated English from 10 source languages, in a European parliament corpus. While they mainly aimed to test translational universals, e.g. simplification, explicitation, etc., the classification accuracy with SVMs using features such as POS trigrams (98%), function words (96%), function word n-grams (100%) provided more evidence that function words and surface syntactic structures may be enough for the identification of translated text.

For Chinese, however, there are very few quantitative studies on translationese (apart from Xiao and Hu, 2015; Hu, 2010, etc.). Xiao and Hu (2015) built a comparable corpus containing 500 original and translated Chinese texts respectively, from four genres. They used statistical tests (log-likelihood tests) to find statistical differences between translated and original Chinese with regard to the frequency of mostly lexical features. They discovered, for example, that translated text use significantly more pronouns than the original texts, across all genres. But they were unable to investigate the syntactic contexts in which those overused pronouns occur most often.

For them, syntactic features were examined through word n-grams, similar to previous studies on Indo-European languages, but no text classification task was carried out.

2.2 Syntactic Features in Text Classification

Although n-gram features are more prevalent in text-classification tasks, deep syntactic features have been found useful as well. In the Native Language Identification (NLI) literature, which in many respects is similar to the task of detecting translations, various forms of context-free grammar (CFG) rules are often used as features (Bykh and Meurers, 2014; Wong and Dras, 2011). Bykh and Meurers (2014) showed that using a form of normalized counts of *lexicalized* CFG rules plus n-grams as features in an ensemble model performed better than all other previous systems. Wong and Dras (2011) reported that using unlexicalized CFG rules (except for function words) from two parsers yielded statistically higher accuracy than simple lexical features (function words, character and POS n-grams).

# texts	news	general prose	science	fiction	total
LCMC	88	206	80	111	485
ZCTC	88	206	80	111	485

Table 1: Distribution of texts across genres

Other approaches have used rules of tree substitution grammar (TSG) (Post and Bergsma, 2013; Swanson and Charniak, 2012) in NLI. Swanson and Charniak (2012) compared the results of CFG rules and two variants of TSG rules and showed that TSG rules obtained through Bayesian methods reached the best results.

Nevertheless, such deep syntactic features are rarely used, if at all, in the identification of translated texts. This is the gap that we hope to fill.

3 Experimental Setup

3.1 Dataset

We use the comparable corpus by Xiao and Hu (2015), which is composed of 500 original Chinese texts from the Lancaster Corpus of Modern Chinese (LCMC), and another 500 human translated Chinese texts from the Zhejiang-University Corpus of Translated Chinese (ZCTC). All texts are of similar lengths (~2000 words), and from different genres. There are four broad genres: news, general prose, science, and fiction (see Table 1), and 15 second-level categories. We exclude texts from the second-level categories "science fiction" and "humor" (both under fiction) since they only have 6 and 9 texts respectively, which is not enough for a classification task.

LCMC (McEnery and Xiao, 2004) was originally designed for "synchronic studies of Chinese and the contrastive studies of Chinese and English" (see Xiao and Hu, 2015, chapter 4.2). It includes written Chinese sampled from 1989 to 1993, amounting to about one million words. ZCTC was created specifically for translation studies "as a comparable counterpart of translated Chinese" to LCMC (Xiao and Hu, 2015, pp. 48), with the same genre distribution and also one million words in total. The texts in ZCTC are sampled in 2001, all translated by human translators, with 99% originally written in English (pp. 50).

Both corpora contain texts that are segmented and POS tagged, processed by the corpus developers using the 2008 version of ICTCLAS (Zhang et al., 2003), a common tagger used in Chinese NLP research. However, only the segmentation is used in this study since our parser uses a different POS tagset.

In this study, we perform 5-fold cross validation on the whole dataset and then evaluate on the full set of 970 texts.

3.2 Pre-Processing and Parser

We remove URLs and headlines, normalize irregular ellipsis (e.g. "。。。", "....") to "......", change all half-width punctuations to full-width, so that our text is compatible with the Chinese Penn Treebank (Xue et al., 2005), which is the training data for the `Stanford CoreNLP` parser (Manning et al., 2014) used in our study.

3.3 Features

Character and word *n*-gram features can be considered upper bound and baseline. On the one hand, they have been used extensively (see Section 2), but on the other hand, they partially encode topic information rather than stylistic differences because of their lexical nature. Consequently, while they are very informative in the current setup, they may not be useful if we want to use the trained model on other texts.

For syntactic features, we use various forms of constituent and dependency parses of the sentences. We extract the following features based on either type of parse using the `CoreNLP` parser with its pre-trained parsing model.

3.3.1 Context-Free Grammar

Context-free grammar rules (CFGR) We use the count of each CFG rule extracted from the parse trees.

Subtrees Subtrees are defined as any part of the constituent tree of any depth, closely following the data-oriented parsing (DOP) paradigm (Bod et al., 2003; Goodman, 1998). Our features differ from the DOP model as well as TSG (Post and Gildea,

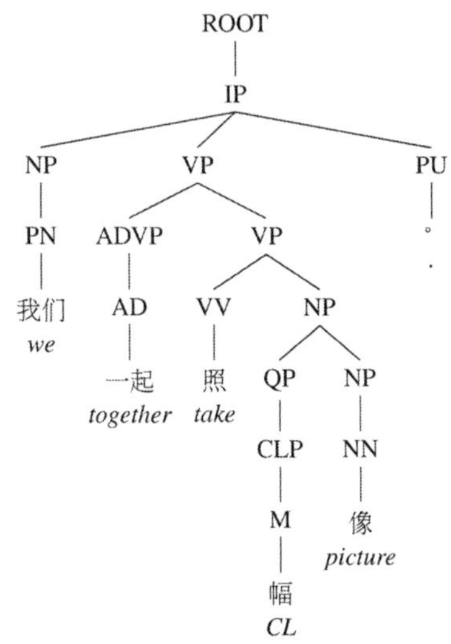

Figure 1: Example constituent tree of the Chinese sentence meaning *We take a picture together*

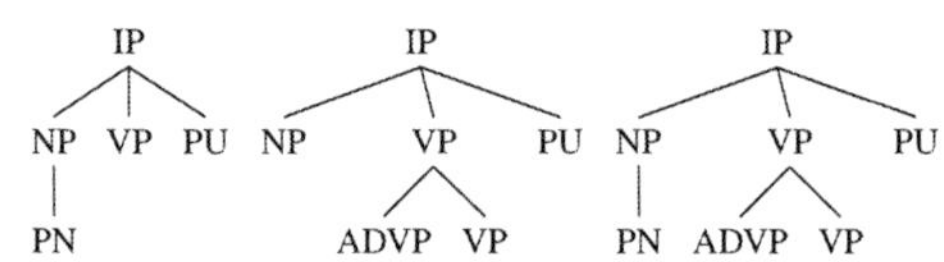

Figure 2: All subtrees of depth 2 with root IP in the tree from Figure 1

2009; Sangati and Zuidema, 2011; Swanson and Charniak, 2012) in that we do not include any lexical information in order to exclude topical influence from content words. Thus no lexical rules are considered, and POS tags are considered to be the leaf nodes (Figure 2).

We experiment with subtrees of depth up to 3 since the number of subtrees grows exponentially as the depth increases. With depth 3, we are already facing more than 1 billion features. Performing subtree extraction and feature selection becomes difficult and time consuming. Also note that CFGRs are essentially subtrees of depth 1. So with increasing maximum depth of subtrees, we test fewer local relations in constituent parses. In the future, we plan to use Bayesian methods (Post and Gildea, 2009) to sample from all the subtrees.

We also conduct separate experiments using subtrees headed by a specific label (we only look at NP, VP, IP, and CP, since they are the most frequent types of subtrees). For example, using NP subtrees as features will inform us how important the noun phrase structure is in identifying translationese.

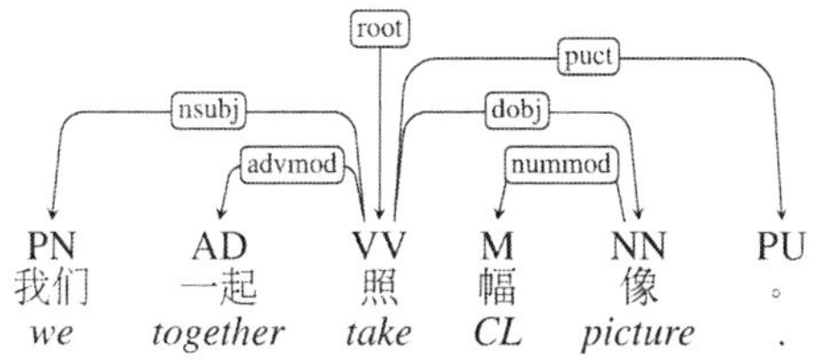

Figure 3: Example dependency graph

3.3.2 Dependency Graphs

Dependency relations, as well as the head and dependent are extracted to construct the following features.

depTriple We combine the POS of a head and its dependent along with the dependency relation, e.g., [VV, nsubj, PN] describes a dependency relation of a nominal subject (nsubj) between a verb (VV) and a pronoun (PN).

depPOS Here only the POS tags of the head and dependent are used, e.g., [VV, PN].

depLabel Only the dependency relation, e.g., [nsubj].

depTripleFuncLex Same as depTriple, except when the word is a function word, we use the lexical item instead of the POS. e.g. [VV, nsubj, 我们] where "我们" (*we*) is a function word (Figure 3).

It should be noted that no lexical information are included in our syntactic features, except for the function words in depTripleFuncLex.

3.3.3 Combination of Features

If combined feature sets work significantly better than one feature set alone, we can draw the conclusion that they model different characteristics of translationese. We experiment with combination of CFGR/subtree and depTriple features.

3.4 Classifier and Feature Selection

For the machine learning experiments, we use support vector machines, in the implementation of the svm.SVC classifier in scikit-learn (Pedregosa et al., 2011). We perform 5-fold cross validation and average over the results. When extracting the folds, we perform stratified sampling across genres so that both training and test data are balanced. Since the number of CFGR/subtree features is much greater than the number of training texts, we perform feature selection by filtering using information gain (Liu et al., 2016; Wong and Dras, 2011) to choose the most discriminative features. Information gain has been shown to select highly discriminative, frequent features for similar tasks (Liu et al., 2014). We experiment with different numbers of features, ranging between the values of 100, 1 000, 10 000, and 50 000.

Features	F-measure (%)
char n-grams(1-3)	95.3
word n-grams(1-3)	94.3
POS n-grams(1-3)	93.9

Table 2: Results for the lexical and POS features

4 Results

4.1 Empirical Evaluation

First we report the results based on lexical and POS features in Table 2 (F-measure).

Character *n*-grams perform the best, achieving an F-measure of 95.3%, followed by word n-grams with an F-measure of 94.3%. Both settings include content words that indicate the source language. In fact, out of the top 30 character n-gram features that predict translations, 4 are punctuations, e.g., the first and family name delimiter "·" in the translations of English names and parentheses "（）"; 11 are function words, e.g. "的" (particle), "可能" (*maybe*), "在" (*in/at*), and many pronouns (*he, I, it, she, they*); all others are content words, where "斯" (*s*) and "尔" (*r*) are at the very top, mainly because they are common transliterations of foreign names involving "s" and "r", followed by "公司" (*company*), "美国" (*US*), "英国" (*UK*), etc. Lexical features have been extensively analyzed in Xiao and Hu (2015), and they reveal little concerning syntactic styles of translated text; thus we will refrain from analyzing them here.

POS *n*-grams also produce good results (F-measure of 93.9%), confirming previous research on Indo-European languages (Baroni and Bernardini, 2005; Koppel and Ordan, 2011). Since they are not lexicalized and thus avoid a topical bias, they provide a better comparison to syntactic features.

Syntactic features: Table 3 presents the result for the syntactic features described in Section 3.3. The best performing unlexicalized syntactic features can reliably classify texts into "original" and "translated", with F-measures greater than 90%,

Features	F (%)
Unlexicalized syntactic features	
CFGR	90.2
subtrees: depth 2	90.9
subtrees: depth 3	92.2
depTriple	91.2
depPOS	89.9
depLabel	89.5
depTripleFuncLex	93.8
Combinations of syntactic features	
CFGR + depTriple	90.5
subtree_d2 + depTriple	91.0
POS n-grams + unlex syn features	
POS + subtree_d2	93.6
POS + depTriple	93.4
POS + subtree_d2 + depTriple	93.8
Char n-grams + unlex syn features	
char + subtree + depTriple	94.4
char + pos + subtree + depTriple	95.5

Table 3: Classification based on syntactic features

Features	F (%)
CFGR NP	86.4
CFGR VP	85.6
CFGR IP	86.6
CFGR CP	68.4
subtrees NP d2	86.0
subtrees VP d2	85.6
subtrees IP d2	89.0
subtrees CP d2	71.6
subtrees NP d3	83.6
subtrees VP d3	86.7
subtrees IP d3	86.9
subtrees CP d3	77.7

Table 4: Results for individual subtrees

which are close to the performance of the purely lexicalized features in Table 2. This suggests that although lexical features do achieve slightly better results, syntactic features alone can capture most of the differences between original and translated texts.

Note that when we increase the depth of constituent parses from 1 (CFGR) to subtrees of depth 3, the F-measure increases by 2 percent, which is a highly significant difference (McNemar (McNemar, 1947) on the 0.001 level). Thus, including deeper constituent information proves helpful in detecting the syntactic styles of texts.

However, combination of different types of syntactic features does not increase the accuracy over the dependency results. Adding syntactic features to POS n-gram or character n-gram features decreases the POS n-gram results slightly, thus indicating that both types of features cover the same information, and POS n-grams are a good approximation of shallow syntax. The lack of improvement when adding syntactic features may also be attributed to their unlexicalized nature in this study. Our syntactic features are completely unlexicalized, whereas research in NLI has shown that CFGR features need to include at least the function words to give higher accuracy (Wong and Dras, 2011). Although this suggests that in terms of classification accuracy, unlexicalized syntactic features cannot provide more information than n-gram features, we can still draw some very interesting observations about styles of translated and original texts, many of which are not possible with simple n-gram features. We will discuss those in the following sections.

4.2 Constituency Features

The top ranking CFG features are shown in Table 5. The top three features in translated section (bottom half) of the table tell us that pronouns (PN) and determiners (DT) are indicative of translated text. We will discuss pronouns in Section 5; as for determiners, dependency graph features in Table 7 further show that among them, "该" (*this*), "这些" (*these*) and "那些" (*those*) are the most prominent. The parenthesis rule (PRN) captures another common feature of translation, i.e., giving the original English form of proper nouns ("加州大学洛杉矶分校（UCLA）") or putting translator's notes in parentheses. Furthermore, the prominence of the two rules `NP → DNP NP` and `DNP → NP DEG` in translation indicates that when an NP is modified by another NP, translators tend to add the particle "的" (DE; DEG for DE Genitive) between the two NPs, for example:

- (NP (DNP (NP 美国) (DEG 的)) (NP 政治)). Gloss: "US DE politics", i.e. US politics
- (NP (DNP (NP 舆论) (DEG 的)) (NP 谴责)). Gloss: "media DE criticism", i.e. criticism from the media
- (NP (DNP (NP 脑) (DEG 的)) (NP 供血)). Gloss: "brain DE blood supply", i.e. cerebral circulation

In all three cases above, "的" can be dropped, and the phrases remain grammatical. But there are

Rank	CFGR	Predicts
2.0	VP → VP PU VP	original
5.0	VP → VP PU VP PU VP	original
10.0	NP → NN	original
10.2	NP → NN PU NN	original
13.6	IP → NP PU VP	original
14.8	NP → NN NN	original
15	NP → ADJP NP	original
16.6	IP → NP PU VP PU	original
18.2	VP → VV	original
19.6	VP → VV NP	original
1.0	NP → PN	translated
4.0	NP → DP NP	translated
6.2	DP → DT	translated
6.6	IP → NP VP PU	translated
6.8	PRN → PU NP PU	translated
6.8	NP → NR	translated
10.0	CP → ADVP IP	translated
10.6	NP → DNP NP	translated
16.4	ADVP → CS	translated
16.8	DNP → NP DEG	translated

Table 5: Top 20 CFGR features; rank averaged across 5-fold CV

Rank	NP CFGR	Predicts
2.0	NP → NN	original
4.0	NP → NN NN	original
5.4	NP → NN **PU** NN	original
6.2	NP → ADJP NP	original
9.8	NP → NN **PU** NN **PU** NN	original
9.8	NP → NP ADJP NP	original
12.2	NP → NP PU NP	original
12.6	NP → NN NN NN	original
14.6	NP → NP NP	original
17.0	NP → NP QP NP	original
18.4	NP → QP NP	original
1.0	NP → PN	translated
4.2	NP → DP NP	translated
6.0	NP → NR	translated
7.2	NP → DNP NP	translated
14.4	NP → QP DNP NP	translated
16.2	NP → NP PRN	translated
16.2	NP → NR **CC** NR	translated
18.2	NP → NP **CC** NP	translated

Table 6: Top 20 NP features (PN: pronoun; NR: proper N; CC: coordinating conjunction)

many cases where "的" is mandatory in the "NP modifying NP" structure. Thus, it is easier to use "的", since it is almost always grammatical, but decisions when to drop "的" are much more subtle. Translators seem to make the safer decision by always using the particle after the NP modifiers, thus making the structure more frequent.

Now we turn to features of subtrees rooted in specific syntactic categories. The classification results are shown in Table 4. Using only NP-headed rules gives us an F-measure of 86.4%. Larger subtrees fare slightly worse, probably indicating data sparsity. However, these results mean that noun phrases alone often provide enough information whether the text is translated.

Table 6 shows the top 20 CFGR features headed by an NP. This gives us an idea of the distinctive structures of noun phrases in original and translated texts. Apart from the obvious over-use of pronouns (PN) and determiner phrases (DP) for NPs in translated text, there are other very interesting patterns: For original Chinese, nouns inside a complex noun phrase tend to be conjoined by a Chinese specific punctuation "、"(similar to the comma in "I like apples, oranges, bananas, etc."), indicated by the high ranking of NP rules involving PU. This punctuation is most often used to separate elements in a list, and a check using `Tregex` (Levy and Andrew, 2006) for the parsed sentences retrieves many phrases like the following from the LCMC corpus: "全院医生、护士最先挖掘的..." (*doctors, nurses from the hospital first dug out...*). In contrast, in translated Chinese, those nouns are more likely to be conjoined by a conjunction (CC), exemplified by the following example from the ZCTC corpus: "对经济**和**股市非常敏感" (*very sensitive to the economy **and** the stock market.*). Here, to conjoin doctors and nurses, or the economy and the stock market, either "、" or "*and*" is grammatical, but original texts favor the former while the translated text, probably influenced by English, prefers the conjunction.

4.3 Dependency Features

Features based on dependency parses have similar F-measures, but should be easier to obtain than subtrees of depth greater than 1. Using the lexical items for function words (depTripleFuncLex) can further improve the results, showing that the choice of function words is indeed very indicative of translationese. A selection of top ranking depTripleFuncLex features is shown in Table 7.

Chinese-specific punctuations such as "、" predicts original Chinese text, as we have already seen, but notice that it is also often used to conjoin verbs (VV_PUNCT_、). Translated texts, in contrast, use more determiners (*these*, *such*, *those*,

Rank	Feature	Predicts	Gloss
1.0	VV_CONJ_VV	original	
2.4	VV_PUNCT_，	original	
2.6	NN_PUNCT_、	original	
4.8	VV_PUNCT_、	original	
11.0	NN_CONJ_NN	original	
18.0	NN_DET_各	original	each
21.4	VA_PUNCT_，	original	
25.0	NN_ETC_等	original	etc.
28.2	VV_PUNCT_：	original	
33.2	VV_PUNCT_！	original	
39.0	NN_DEP_三	original	three
41.2	NN_DET_全	original	all
42.6	VA_**NSUBJ**_NN	original	
77.2	VV_DOBJ_NN	original	
94.8	VV_**NSUBJ**_NN	original	
5.4	VV_**NSUBJ**_我	translated	I
8.2	VV_ADVMOD_将	translated	will
10.0	VV_**NSUBJ**_他	translated	he
10.2	NN_DET_该	translated	this
11.6	NN_DET_这些	translated	these
14.0	NR_CASE_的	translated	DE
17.0	VV_**NSUBJ**_他们	translated	they
24.0	VV_**NSUBJ**_她	translated	she
27.6	他_CASE_的	translated	his
29.6	NN_NMOD:ASSMOD_他	translated	he
31.0	VV_PUNCT_。	translated	period
33.6	VV_ADVMOD_但是	translated	but
35.6	VV_**NSUBJ**_你	translated	you
35.8	VV_ADVMOD_如果	translated	if
37.6	VV_MARK_的	translated	DE
37.8	NN_DET_任何	translated	any
40.6	VV_CASE_因为	translated	because
41.2	NR_CC_和	translated	and
44	NN_DET_那些	translated	those
47.2	VV_NSUBJ_它	translated	it
191.0	VV_DOBJ_它	translated	it

Table 7: Top depTripleFuncLex features

Rank	Feature	Function
1.0	(NP **PN**)	NA
2.2	(IP (NP **PN**) VP)	Subj.
5.2	(DNP (NP **PN**) DEG)	Genitive
6.6	(IP (NP **PN**) VP PU)	Subj.
38.0	(IP (NP **PN**) (VP VV VP))	Subj.
56.0	(IP (NP **PN**) (VP ADVP VP))	Subj.
77.0	(IP (ADVP) (NP **PN**) VP)	Subj.
81.0	(IP (NP **PN**) (VP ADVP VP) PU)	Subj.
81.0	(IP (ADVP AD) (NP **PN**) (VP)	Subj.
93.5	(PP P (NP **PN**)	Obj. of prep.
93.5	(IP (NP **PN**) (VP (VV IP))	Subj.
93.6	(VP VV (NP **PN**) IP)	Obj. of verb

Table 8: Top subtree (depth=2) features involving pronouns (PN)

each, etc.) and pronouns (*he*, *they*, etc.), which will be discussed in more detail in the following section. These results are in accordance with previous research on translationese in Chinese (He, 2008; Xiao and Hu, 2015).

5 Analyzing Features: Pronouns

In this section, we discuss one example where syntactic features provide unique information about the stylistic differences between original and translated Chinese that cannot be extracted from lexical sequences, yielding new insights into translationese in Chinese: We have a closer look at the use of pronouns. For this investigation, we examine the top 100 subtrees with depth 2, selected by information gain.

Our results not only confirm the previous finding that pronoun usage is more prominent in translated Chinese (He, 2008; Xiao and Hu, 2015, among others, see Section 2.1), but also provide more insights on the details of pronoun usage in translated Chinese, by looking at the syntactic structures that involve a pronoun (PN) and their ranking after applying the feature ranking algorithm (see Table 8).

The high ranking of pronoun-related features (4 out of the top 10 features involve pronouns) confirms the distinguishing power of pronoun usage. Crucially, it appears that pronouns in subject position or as a genitive (as part of DNP phrase such as 他的书, *his book*), are more prominent than pronoun in the object position in translated texts. In fact, pronouns as the object of a preposition (captured by subtree "(PP P (NP PN))") ranked only about 93rd among all features. Also, pronouns as the object of a verb only shows up once in the top 100 features, and they are of the structure "(VP VV (NP PN) IP)". When searching for sentences with such structures (using Tregex), we almost always encounter phrases similar to "make + pronoun + V.", e.g. "让 他们 懂得 ..." (*make them understand ...*), where the pronoun is both the object of "make", and the subject of "understand". All this shows that the over-usage of pronouns in translated texts is more likely to occur in subject positions, or in a genitive complement, rather than as the direct object of a verb. Even when it appears in the object position, it appears to play both the roles of subject and object. To our knowledge, this characteristic has not been discussed in previous studies in translationese.

If we examine the dependency features, we see the same pattern. Pronouns serving as the subject of verbs rank very high (5.4, 10, 17, 24, 35.6, see Table 7), whereas pronouns as the object of verbs are not in the top 100 features (the highest ranking 191, VV_DOBJ_它 *it*). Thus we see the two types of syntactic features (constituent trees and dependency trees) converging to the same conclusion. If we look at the pronoun issue from the opposite side, a reasonable consequence would be that in original texts, more common nouns should serve as the subject, which is indeed what we find. VV_NSUBJ_NN predicts "original" and ranks 94.8.

The conclusion concerning pronoun usage drawn from the ranking of syntactic features coincides with observation of (non-)pro-drop in English and Chinese. I.e., Chinese is pro-drop while Enlgish is not. Thus, the overuse of pronouns in Chinese texts translated from English is an example of the interference effect (Toury, 1979), where translators are likely to carry over linguistic features in the source language to the target language. A further observation is that, in Chinese, subject pro-drop seems to be more frequent. The reason is that subject pro-drop does not require much context, while object-drop generally requires the dropped object to be discourse old (c.f. Li and Thompson, 1981). This explains why pronoun overuse occurs more often in subject position in translated text, because object pro-drop in Chinese itself is less common in original Chinese text.

We are not trying to imply that lexical features should not be used. Rather, we want to stress that syntactic features offer a more in-depth and comprehensive picture to linguists interested in the style of translated text. The pronoun analysis presented above is only one such example. We can perform such analyses for any feature of interest and gain a deeper understanding of how they occur in both types of text.

6 Conclusion and Future Work

To our knowledge, the current study is the first machine learning experiment on translated vs. original Chinese. We find that translationese can be identified with roughly the same high accuracy using either lexical n-gram features or syntactic features. More importantly, we show how syntactic features can yield linguistically meaningful features that can help decipher differences in styles of translated and original texts. For example, translated Chinese features more determiners, subject-position pronouns, NP modifiers involving "的", and multiple NPs or VPs conjoined by the Chinese-specific punctuation "、". Our methodology can, in principle, be applied to any stylistic comparisons in the digital humanities, and can yield stylistic insights much deeper than the pioneering work of Mosteller and Wallace (1963).

In future work, we will investigate tree substitution grammar (TSG), which extracts even deeper constituent trees (c.f. Post and Gildea, 2009), and detailed feature interpretation for phrases headed by other tags (ADJP, PP, etc.) and for specific genres. It is also desirable to improve the accuracy of constituent parsers for Chinese, along the lines of (Wang et al., 2013; Wang and Xue, 2014; Hu et al., 2017), since accurate syntactic trees are the prerequisite for accurate feature interpretation. While the parser in this study works well, better parsers will undoubtedly be a plus.

Acknowledgement

We thank Ruoze Huang, Jiahui Huang and Chien-Jer Charles Lin for helpful discussions, and the anonymous reviewers for their suggestions. Hai Hu is funded by China Scholarship Council.

References

Marco Baroni and Silvia Bernardini. 2005. A new approach to the study of translationese: Machine-learning the difference between original and translated text. *Literary and Linguistic Computing* 21(3):259–274.

Rens Bod, Remko Scha, Khalil Sima'an, et al. 2003. *Data-oriented parsing*. CSLI Publications.

Serhiy Bykh and Detmar Meurers. 2014. Exploring syntactic features for native language identification: A variationist perspective on feature encoding and ensemble optimization. In *Proceedings of COLING 2014, the 25th International Conference on Computational Linguistics*. pages 1962–1973.

Joshua Goodman. 1998. *Parsing inside-out*. Ph.D. thesis, Harvard University.

Yang He. 2008. *A Study of Grammatical Features in Europeanized Chinese*. Commercial Press.

Hai Hu, Daniel Dakota, and Sandra Kübler. 2017. Non-deterministic segmentation for chinese lattice parsing. In *Proceedings of the International Conference Recent Advances in Natural Language Processing, RANLP 2017*. pages 316–324.

Xianyao Hu. 2010. A corpus-based multi-dimensional analysis of the stylistic features of translated chinese (in chinese). *Foreign Language Teaching and Research* 42(6):451–458.

Iustina Ilisei, Diana Inkpen, Gloria Corpas Pastor, and Ruslan Mitkov. 2010. Identification of translationese: A machine learning approach. In *CICLing*. Springer, volume 6008, pages 503–511.

Moshe Koppel and Noam Ordan. 2011. Translationese and its dialects. In *Proceedings of the 49th Annual Meeting of the ACL: HLT*. pages 1318–1326.

Gennadi Lembersky, Noam Ordan, and Shuly Wintner. 2012. Language models for machine translation: Original vs. translated texts. *Computational Linguistics* 38(4):799–825.

Roger Levy and Galen Andrew. 2006. Tregex and Tsurgeon: Tools for querying and manipulating tree data structures. In *Proceedings of the Fifth International Conference on Language Resources and Evaluation*. pages 2231–2234.

Charles Li and Sandra Thompson. 1981. *A functional reference grammar of Mandarin Chinese*. Berkeley: University of California Press.

Can Liu, Sandra Kübler, and Ning Yu. 2014. Feature selection for highly skewed sentiment analysis tasks. In *Proceedings of the Second Workshop on Natural Language Processing for Social Media (SocialNLP)*. Dublin, Ireland, pages 2–11.

Can Liu, Wen Li, Bradford Demarest, Yue Chen, Sara Couture, Daniel Dakota, Nikita Haduong, Noah Kaufman, Andrew Lamont, Manan Pancholi, et al. 2016. IUCL at SemEval-2016 task 6: An ensemble model for stance detection in twitter. In *Proceedings of the 10th International Workshop on Semantic Evaluation (SemEval)*. pages 394–400.

Christopher Manning, Mihai Surdeanu, John Bauer, Jenny Finkel, Steven J. Bethard, and David McClosky. 2014. The Stanford CoreNLP Natural Language Processing Toolkit. In *Association for Computational Linguistics (ACL) System Demonstrations*. pages 55–60.

Anthony McEnery and Zhonghua Xiao. 2004. The Lancaster Corpus of Mandarin Chinese: A corpus for monolingual and contrastive language study. *Religion* 17:3–4.

Quinn McNemar. 1947. Note on the sampling error of the difference between correlated proportions or percentages. *Psychometrika* 12(2):153–157.

Frederick Mosteller and David L Wallace. 1963. Inference in an authorship problem: A comparative study of discrimination methods applied to the authorship of the disputed Federalist Papers. *Journal of the American Statistical Association* 58(302):275–309.

F. Pedregosa, G. Varoquaux, A. Gramfort, V. Michel, B. Thirion, O. Grisel, M. Blondel, P. Prettenhofer, R. Weiss, V. Dubourg, J. Vanderplas, A. Passos, D. Cournapeau, M. Brucher, M. Perrot, and E. Duchesnay. 2011. Scikit-learn: Machine learning in Python. *Journal of Machine Learning Research* 12:2825–2830.

Matt Post and Shane Bergsma. 2013. Explicit and implicit syntactic features for text classification. In *Proceedings of the 51st Annual Meeting of the Association for Computational Linguistics*. volume 2, pages 866–872.

Matt Post and Daniel Gildea. 2009. Bayesian learning of a tree substitution grammar. In *Proceedings of the ACL-IJCNLP 2009 Conference*. pages 45–48.

Federico Sangati and Willem Zuidema. 2011. Accurate parsing with compact tree-substitution grammars: Double-DOP. In *Proceedings of the Conference on Empirical Methods in Natural Language Processing*. pages 84–95.

Ben Swanson and Eugene Charniak. 2012. Native language detection with tree substitution grammars. In *Proceedings of the 50th Annual Meeting of the ACL*. pages 193–197.

Gideon Toury. 1979. Interlanguage and its manifestations in translation. *Meta: Journal des traducteurs/Meta: Translators' Journal* 24(2):223–231.

Vered Volansky, Noam Ordan, and Shuly Wintner. 2013. On the features of translationese. *Digital Scholarship in the Humanities* 30(1):98–118.

Zhiguo Wang and Nianwen Xue. 2014. Joint POS tagging and transition-based constituent parsing in Chinese with non-local features. In *Proceedings of the 52nd Annual Meeting of the Association for Computational Linguistics*. volume 1, pages 733–742.

Zhiguo Wang, Chengqing Zong, and Nianwen Xue. 2013. A lattice-based framework for joint Chinese word segmentation, POS tagging and parsing. In *Proceedings of the 51st Annual Meeting of the Association for Computational Linguistics*. volume 2, pages 623–627.

Sze-Meng Jojo Wong and Mark Dras. 2011. Exploiting parse structures for native language identification. In *Proceedings of the Conference on Empirical Methods in Natural Language Processing*. pages 1600–1610.

Richard Xiao and Xianyao Hu. 2015. *Corpus-Based Studies of Translational Chinese in English-Chinese Translation*. Springer.

Naiwen Xue, Fei Xia, Fu-Dong Chiou, and Marta Palmer. 2005. The Penn Chinese TreeBank: Phrase structure annotation of a large corpus. *Natural Language Engineering* 11(2):207–238.

Huaping Zhang, Hongkui Yu, Deyi Xiong, and Qun Liu. 2003. HHMM-based Chinese lexical analyzer ICTCLAS. In *Proceedings of the Second SIGHAN Workshop on Chinese Language Processing*. pages 184–187.

Evaluating Creative Language Generation: The Case of Rap Lyric Ghostwriting

Peter Potash, Alexey Romanov, Anna Rumshisky
Department of Computer Science
University of Massachusetts Lowell
{ppotash,aromanov,arum}@cs.uml.edu

Abstract

Language generation tasks that seek to mimic human ability to use language creatively are difficult to evaluate, since one must consider creativity, style, and other non-trivial aspects of the generated text. The goal of this paper is to develop evaluations methods for one such task, ghostwriting of rap lyrics, and to provide an explicit, quantifiable foundation for the goals and future directions for this task. Ghostwriting must produce text that is similar in style to the emulated artist, yet distinct in content. We develop a novel evaluation methodology that addresses several complementary aspects of this task, and illustrate how such evaluation can be used to meaningfully analyze system performance. We provide a corpus of lyrics for 13 rap artists, annotated for stylistic similarity, which allows us to assess the feasibility of manual evaluation for generated verse.

1 Introduction

Language generation tasks are often among the most difficult to evaluate. Evaluating machine translation, image captioning, summarization, and other similar tasks is typically done via comparison with existing human-generated "references". However, human beings also use language creatively, and for the language generation tasks that seek to mimic this ability, determining how accurately the generated text represents its target is insufficient, as one also needs to evaluate creativity and style. We believe that one of the reasons such tasks receive little attention is the lack of sound evaluation methodology, without which no task is well-defined, and no progress can be made. The goal of this paper is to develop an evaluation methodology for one such task, ghostwriting, or more specifically, ghostwriting of rap lyrics.

Ghostwriting is ubiquitous in politics, literature, and music; as such, it introduces a distinction between the performer/presenter of text, lyrics, etc, and the creator of text/lyrics. The goal of ghostwriting is to present something in a style that is believable enough to be credited to the performer. In the domain of rap specifically, rappers sometimes function as ghostwriters early on before embarking on their own public careers, and there are even businesses that provide written lyrics as a service[1]. The goal of automatic ghostwriting is therefore to create a system that can take as input a given artist's work and generate **similar** yet **unique** lyrics.

Our objective in this work is to provide a quantifiable direction and foundation for the task of rap lyric generation and similar tasks through (1) developing an evaluation methodology for such models and (2) illustrating how such evaluation can be used to analyze system performance, including advantages and limitations of a specific language model developed for this task. As an illustration case, we use the ghostwriter model previously proposed in exploratory work by Potash et al. (2015), which uses a recurrent neural network (RNN) with Long Short-Term Memory (LSTM) for rap lyric generation.

The following are the main contributions of this paper. We present a comprehensive manual evaluation methodology of the generated verses along three key aspects: fluency, coherence, and style matching. We introduce an improvement to the semi-automatic methodology used by Potash et al. (2015) that automatically penalizes repetitive text, removing the need for manual intervention. Finally, we build a corpus of lyrics for 13 rap artists, each with his own unique style, and conduct a comprehensive evaluation of the LSTM model performance using the new evaluation methodol-

[1] http://www.rap-rebirth.com/, http://www.precisionwrittens.com/rap-ghostwriters-for-hire/

Proceedings of the 2nd Workshop on Stylistic Variation, pages 29–38
New Orleans, Louisiana, June 5, 2018.

ogy. The corpus includes style matching annotation for select verses in dataset, which can form a gold standard for future work on automatic representation of similarity between artists' styles. The resulting rap lyric dataset is publicly available from the authors' website[2].

Additionally, we believe that the annotation method we propose for manual style evaluation can be used for other similar generation tasks. One example is 'Deep Art' work in the computer vision community that seeks to apply the style of a particular painting to other images (Gatys et al., 2015; Li and Wand, 2016). Although manual inspection of results of such models suggests reasonable success, a systemic evaluation methodology has yet to be proposed. With this in mind, we make the interface used for style evaluation in this work available for public use.

Our evaluation results highlight the truly multi-faceted nature of the ghostwriting task. While having a single measure of success is clearly desirable, our analysis shows the need for complementary metrics that evaluate different components of the overall task. Indeed, despite the fact that our test-case LSTM model outperforms a baseline model across numerous artists based on automated evaluation, the full set of evaluation metrics is able to showcase the LSTM model's strengths and weakness. The coherence evaluation demonstrates the difficulty of incorporating large amounts of training data into the LSTM model, which intuitively would be desirable to create a flexible ghostwriting model. The style matching experiments suggest that the LSTM is effective at capturing an artist's general style, however, this may indicate that it tends to form 'average' verses, which are then more likely to be matched with existing verses from an artist rather than another random verse from the same artist. Overall, the evaluation methodology we present provides an explicit, quantifiable foundation for the ghostwriting task, allowing for a deeper understanding of the task's goals and future research directions.

2 Related Work

Previous work that explores text generation for artistic purposes, such as poetry and lyrics, generally uses either automated or manual evaluation. We would like to point out that none of the works discussed below implement models that generate complete verses from scratch (including verse structure), which is the goal of the models we aim to evaluate. In terms of manual evaluation, Barbieri et al. (2012) have a set of annotators evaluate generated lyrics along two separate dimensions: grammar and semantic relatedness to song title. The annotators rate the dimensions with scores 1-3. A similar strategy is used by Gervás (2000), where the author has annotators evaluate generated verses with regard to syntactic correctness and overall aesthetic value, providing scores in the range 1-5. Wu et al. (2013) have annotators determine the effectiveness of various systems based on fluency as well as rhyming. Some heuristic-based automated approaches have also been used, e.g., by Oliveira et al. (2014) who use a simple automatic heuristic that awards lines for ending in a termination previously used in the generated stanza. Malmi et al. (2015) evaluate their generated lyrics based on the verses' rhyme density, on the assumption that a higher rhyme density means better lyrics.

3 Dataset

For our evaluation experiments, we selected the following list of artists in four different categories:

- Three top-selling rap artists according to Wikipedia[3]: Eminem, Jay Z, Tupac
- Artists with the largest vocabulary according to Pop Chart Lab[4]: Aesop Rock, GZA, Sage Francis
- Artists with the smallest vocabulary according to Pop Chart Lab: DMX, Drake
- Best classified artists from Hirjee and Brown (2010b) using rhyme detection features[5]: Fabolous, Nototious B.I.G., Lil' Wayne

We collected all available songs from the above artists from the site *The Original Hip-Hop (Rap) Lyrics Archive - OHHLA.com - Hip-Hop Since 1992*[6]. We removed the metadata, line repetiton markup, and chorus lines, and tokenized the lyrics

[2] `http://text-machine.cs.uml.edu/ghostwriter/`

[3] `http://en.wikipedia.org/wiki/List_of_best-selling_music_artists`

[4] `http://popchartlab.com/products/the-hip-hop-flow-chart`

[5] Specifically, the authors used their automated rhyme detection tool to generate rhyme statistics of verses, and used those rhyme features, along with more shallow features such as syllable count and word repetition, to classify the artist of the verse.

[6] `http://www.ohhla.com/`

using the NLTK library (Bird et al., 2009). Since the preprocessing was done heuristically, the resulting dataset may still contain some text that is not actual verse, but rather dialogue or chorus lines. We therefore filter out all verses that are shorter than 20 tokens. Statistics of our dataset are shown in Table 1.

4 Evaluation Methodology

We believe that adequate evaluation for the ghostwriting task requires both manual and automatic approaches. The automated evaluation methodology enables large-scale analysis of the generated verse. However, given the nature of the task, the automated evaluation is not able to assess certain critical aspects of fluency and style, such as the vocabulary, the tone, and the themes preferred by a particular artist. In this section, we present a manual methodology we propose for evaluating these aspects of the generated verse, as well as an improvement to the automatic methodology proposed by Potash et al. (2015).

4.1 Manual Evaluation

We have designed two annotation tasks for manual evaluation. The first task is to determine how fluent and coherent the generated verses are. The second task is to evaluate manually how well the generated verses match the style of the target artist.

Fluency/Coherence Evaluation Given a generated verse, we ask annotators to determine the fluency and coherence of the lyrics. Even though our evaluation is for systems that produce entire verses, we follow the work of Wu (2014) and annotate fluency, as well as coherence, at the line level. To assess fluency, we ask to what extent a given line can be considered a valid English utterance. Since a language model may produce highly disjointed verses as it progresses through the training process, we offer the annotator three options for grading fluency: strongly fluent, weakly fluent, and not fluent. If a line is disjointed, i.e., it is only fluent in specific segments of the line, the annotators are instructed to mark it as weakly fluent. The grade of not fluent is reserved for highly incoherent text.

To assess coherence, we ask the annotator how well a given line matches the preceding line. That is, how believable is it that these two lines would follow each other in a rap verse. We offer the annotators the same choices as in the fluency evaluation: strongly coherent, weakly coherent, and not coherent. During the training process, a language model may output the same line repeatedly. We account for this in our coherence evaluation by defining the consecutive repetition of a line as not coherent. This is important to define because the line on its own may be strongly fluent, however, it is not correct to consider a verse that consists of a single fluent line repeated indefinitely to be coherent.

Style Matching The goal of the style matching annotation is to determine how well a given verse captures the style of the target artist. In this annotation task, a user is presented with a verse and asked to compare it against four other verses. The goal is to pick the verse that is written in a similar style. One of the four choices is always a verse from the same artist that was used to generate the verse being evaluated. The other three verses are chosen from the remaining artists in our dataset. Each verse is evaluated in this manner four times, each time against different verses, so that it has the chance to get matched with a verse from each of the remaining twelve artists. The generated verse is considered stylistically consistent if the annotators tend to select the verse that belongs to the target artist. To evaluate the difficulty of this task, we also perform style matching annotation for authentic verse, in which the evaluated verse is not generated, but rather is an actual existing verse from the target artist.[7]

4.2 Automated Evaluation

The automated evaluation we describe below attempts to capture computationally the dual aspects of "unique yet similar" in a manner originally proposed by Potash et al. (2015).

Uniqueness of Generated Lyrics We use a modified tf-idf representation for verses, and calculate cosine similarity between generated verses and the verses from the training data to determine novelty (or lack thereof). In order to determine which training verse a generated verse matches the most, we calculate the maximum similarity score across all training verses.

[7]As mentioned earlier, we believe that this annotation method can be useful for evaluation of a wide range of other style-dependent generation tasks, so we have made the annotation interface available on (`http://text-machine.cs.uml.edu/ghostwriter/`).

Artist	Verses	Unique Vocab	Vocab Richness	Avg Len	Stdev Len	Max Len
Tupac	660	5776	7.1	117	83	423
Aesop Rock	549	11815	14.8	140	139	1039
DMX	819	5593	5.3	125	82	552
Drake	665	6064	7.0	128	112	1057
Eminem	1429	12393	6.2	136	105	931
Fabolous	892	8304	7.4	122	91	662
GZA	287	6845	15.9	145	102	586
Jay Z	1245	9596	6.7	111	81	842
Lil' Wayne	1564	10848	5.5	124	101	977
Nototious B.I.G.	426	5465	10.2	120	88	557
Sage Francis	570	8082	11.9	114	112	645
Kanye West	851	7007	7.6	105	109	2264
Kool Keith	1471	13280	7.4	118	85	626
Too Short	1259	7396	4.3	134	123	1411

Table 1: Rap lyrics dataset statistics. Vocabulary richness measures how varied an artist's vocabulary is, computed as the total number of words divided by vocabulary size.

Stylistic Similarity via Rhyme Density of Lyrics We use the rhyme detection tool provided by Hirjee and Brown (2010a) calculate the rhyme density of a given verse, with the ultimate goal of evaluating how well the generated verse models an artist's style (specifically, rhyme style in this case). The point of an effective system is not to produce arbitrary rhymes: it is to produce rhyme types and rhyme frequency similar to the target artist. For the ghostwriter models trained exclusively on the verses of a given artist, the vocabulary of the generated verse is closed with respect to the training data. In that case, assessing how similar the generated vocabulary is to the target artist is not important. Instead, we focus on rhyme density, which is defined as the number of rhymed syllables divided by the total number of syllables (Hirjee and Brown, 2010a). Certain artists distinguish themselves by having more complicated rhyme schemes, such as the use of internal[8] or polysyllabic rhymes[9]. Rhyme density is able to capture this in a single metric.

However, this rhyme detection method is not designed to deal with highly repetitive text, which the LSTM model produces often in the early stages of training. Since the same phoneme is repeated (because the same word is repeated), the rhyme detection tool generates a false positive. Potash et al. (2015) dealt with this by manually inspecting the rhyme densities of verses generated in the early stages of training to determine if a generated verse should be kept for the evaluation procedure.

In order to fully automate their method, we account for the presence of repetitive text by weighting the rhyme density of a given verse by its entropy. More specifically, for a given verse, we calculate entropy at the token level and divide by total number of tokens in that verse. Verses with highly repetitive text will have a low entropy, which results in down-weighting the rhyme density of verses that produce false positive rhymes due to their repetitive text.

Merging Uniqueness and Similarity Since ghostwriting is a balancing act of the two opposing forces of textual uniqueness and stylistic similarity, we want a low correlation between rhyme density (stylistic similarity) and maximum verse similarity (lack of textual uniqueness). However, our goal is not to have a high rhyme density, but rather to have the rhyme density similar to the target artist, while simultaneously keeping the maximum similarity score low. As the model overfits the training data, both the value of maximum similarity and the rhyme density will increase, until the model generates the original verse directly. Therefore, our goal is to evaluate the value of the maximum similarity at the point where the rhyme density has the value of the target artist. In order to accomplish this, we follow Potash et al. (2015) and plot the values of rhyme density and maximum similarity obtained at different points during model training. We use regression lines for these points to identify the value of the maximum similarity line at the point where the rhyme density line

[8] e.g. "New York City gritty committee pity the fool" and "How I made it you salivated over my calibrated"

[9] e.g. "But it was your op to shop stolen art/Catch a swollen heart form not rolling smart".

has the value of the target artist. We give more detail below.

5 Lyric Generation Experiments

The main generative model we use in our evaluation experiments is an LSTM. Similar to Potash et al. (2015), we use an n-gram model as a baseline system for automated evaluation. We refer the reader to the original work for a detailed description. After every 100 iterations of training[10] the LSTM model generates a verse. For the baseline model, we generate five verses at values 1-9 for n. We see a correspondence between higher n and higher iteration: as both increase, the models become more 'fit' to the training data.

For the baseline model, we use the verses generated at different n-gram lengths ($n = 1...9$) to obtain the values for regression. At every value of n, we take the average rhyme density and maximum similarity score of the five verses that we generate to create a single data point for rhyme density and maximum similarity score, respectively.

To enable comparison, we also create nine data points from the verses generated by the LSTM, which is done as follows: a separate model for each artist is trained for a minimum of 16,400 iterations. We take the verses generated every 2,000 iterations, from 0 to 16,000 iterations, giving us nine points. The averages for each point are obtained by using the verses generated in iterations $\pm x, x \in \{100, 200, 300, 400\}$ for each interval of 2,000.

6 Results

We present the results of our evaluation experiments using both manual evaluation and automated analysis.

6.1 Fluency/Coherence

In order to fairly compare the fluency/coherence of verses across artists, we use the verses generated by each artist's model at 16,000 iterations. We apply the fluency/coherence annotation methodology from Section 4.1. Each line is annotated by two annotators. Annotation results are shown in Figure 2 and Figure 3. For each annotated verse, we report the percentage of lines annotated as strongly fluent, weakly fluent, and not fluent, as well as the corresponding percentages for coherence. We convert the raw annotation results into a single score for each verse by treating the labels "strongly fluent", "weakly fluent", and "not fluent" as numeric values 1, 0.5, and 0, respectively. Treating each annotation on a given line separately, we calculate the average numeric rating for a given verse:

$$Fluency = \frac{\#sf + 0.5\#wf}{\#a} \quad (1)$$

where $\#sf$ is the number of times any line is labeled strongly fluent, $\#wf$ is the number of times any line is labeled weakly fluent, and $\#a$ is the total annotations provided for a verse, which is equal to the number of lines $\times$ 2. *Coherence* is calculated in a similar manner. In terms of practically implementing the annotation methodology, an annotators annotates an average of 8.5 lines per minute (this includes fluency and coherence). For our experiments, it took 3.3 hours to annotate 1,687 lines. A qualitative analysis of fluency/coherence annotation is given in Figure 1.

[10]Training is done in batches with two verses per batch.

what more could i say i wouldn t be here today
if the old school didn t pave the way grand puba

(a) Tupac's generated verse that was evaluated for fluency (0.88) and coherence (1.00). The verse is generally fluent, however, the ending of the second verse represents a break in fluency that results in the line being labeled *weakly fluent*. This break in fluency does not affect the perfect fluency score.

i m gon na be alright or die
i m a dog and i m the dog and i m a dog
but i m gon na be alright
and i m gon na be alright

(b) DMX's generated verse that was evaluated for fluency (0.42) and coherence (0.36). The overall repetitiveness contributes to the verse's lack of coherence, and the second line in particular contributes to the verse's general lack of fluency.

Figure 1: A qualitative analysis of verses annotated for fluency and coherence.

6.2 Style Matching

We performed style-matching annotation for the verses generated at iterations 16,000–16,400 for each artist. Therefore, each artist has five generated verses available for evaluation, one for each interval of 100 iterations. For the experiment with authentic verses, we randomly chose five verses from each artist, with a verse length of at least 40 tokens. Each page was annotated twice, by native English-speaking rap fans. The results of our style

Artist	Authentic			Generated		
	Match%	Match$_A$%	Raw agreement %	Match%	Match$_A$%	Raw agreement %
Tupac	35.0	50.0	40.0	45.0	57.1	35.0
Aesop Rock	30.0	25.0	40.0	37.5	100.0	10.0
DMX	40.0	71.4	35.0	27.5	30.0	50.0
Drake	32.5	44.4	45.0	37.5	40.0	25.0
Eminem	12.5	00.0	50.0	35.0	50.0	30.0
Fabolous	25.0	12.5	40.0	45.0	50.0	40.0
GZA	52.5	72.7	55.0	32.5	22.2	45.0
Jay Z	35.0	42.9	35.0	22.5	22.2	45.0
Lil' Wayne	27.5	22.2	45.0	37.5	57.1	35.0
Notorious B.I.G.	25.0	0.00	35.0	27.5	33.3	30.0
Sage Francis	52.5	66.7	45.0	22.5	16.7	30.0
Average	33.4	37.1	42.3	33.6	43.5	34.1

Table 2: The percentage of correct matches and the inter-annotator agreement in style matching evaluation

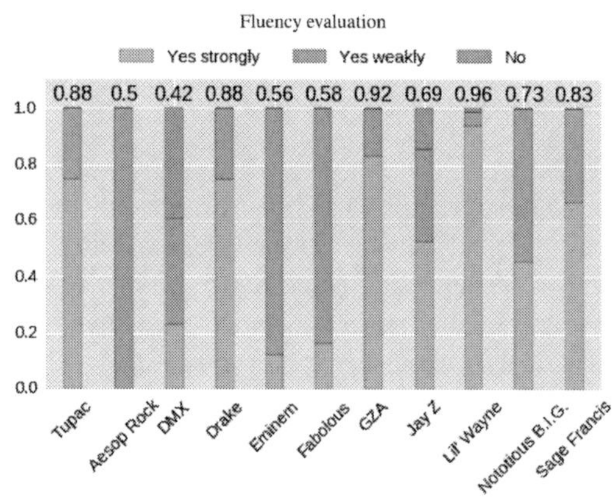

Figure 2: Percentage of lines annotated as strongly fluent, weakly fluent, and not fluent. The numbers above the bars reflect the total score of the artist (higher is better). The resulting mean is 0.723 and the standard deviation is 0.178.

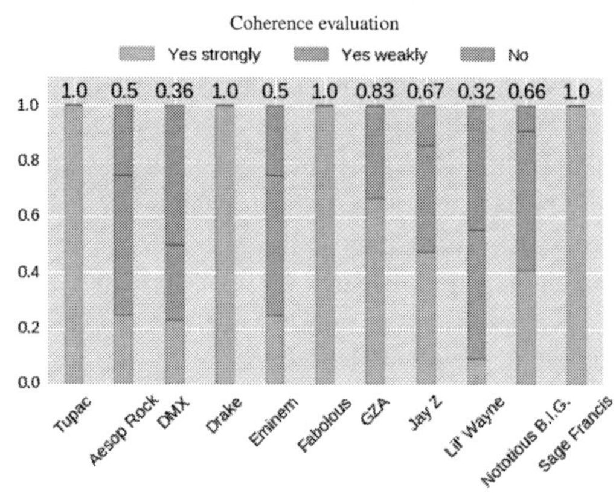

Figure 3: Percentage of lines annotated as strongly coherent, weakly coherent, and not coherent. The numbers above the bars reflect the total score of the artist (higher is better). The resulting mean is 0.713 and the standard deviation is 0.256.

matching annotations are shown in Table 2. We present two different views of the results. First, each annotation for a page is considered separately and we calculate:

$$Match\% = \frac{\#m}{\#a} \quad (2)$$

where $\#m$ is the number of times, on a given page, the chosen verse actually came from the target artist, and $\#a$ is the total number of annotations done. For a given artist, five verses were evaluated, each verse appeared on four separate pages, and each page is annotated twice, so $\#a$ is equal to 40. Since in each case (i.e., page) the classes are different, we cannot use Fleiss' kappa directly. Raw agreement for style annotation, which corresponds to the percentage of times annotators picked the same verse (whether or not they are correct) is shown in the column 'Raw agreement %' in Table 2.

We also report annotators' joint ability to guess the target artist correctly, which we compute as follows:

$$Match_A\% = \frac{\#m_A}{\#s_A} \quad (3)$$

where $\#s_A$ is the number of times the annotators agreed on a verse on the same page, and $\#m_A$ is the number of times that the agreed upon verse is from the target artist.

In terms of times requirements for implementing this annotation task, each page takes two minutes on average to complete, given that the annotator must read five verses then make the match decision. For our experiments, we annotated 880 pages total, resulting in a total annotation time of 29 hours.

6.2.1 Artist Confusion

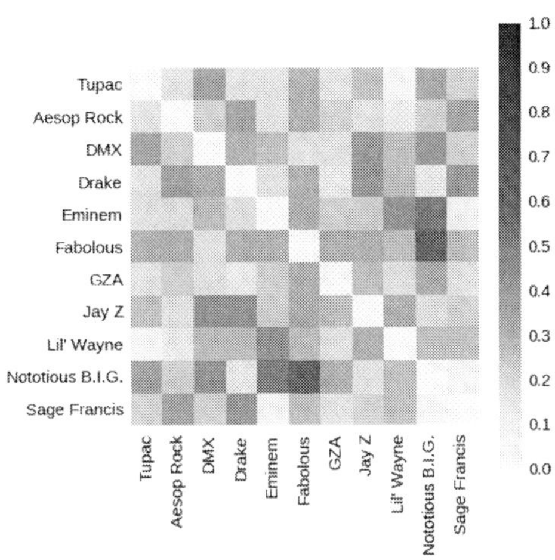

Figure 4: Fraction of confusions between artists

The results of style-matching annotation provides us with an interesting insight into the similarity between two artists' styles. This is captured by the *confusion* between two artists during the annotation of the pages with authentic verses, which is computed as follows:

$$Confusion(a, b) = \frac{\#c(a, b) + \#c(b, a)}{\#p(a, b) + \#p(b, a)} \quad (4)$$

where $\#p(a, b)$ is the number of times a verse from artist a is presented for evaluation and a verse from artist b is shown as one of four choices; $\#c(a, b)$ is the number of times the verse from artist b was chosen as the matching verse. The resulting confusion matrix is presented in Figure 4. We intend for this data to provide a gold standard for future experiments that would attempt to encode the similarity of artists' styles. For example, if we were to try to embed an artist, we could use the confusion results as gold standard similarity scores between the artists' embeddings to determine how effective the embedding methodology is.

6.3 Automated Evaluation

The results of our automated evaluation are shown in Table 3. For each artist, we calculate their average rhyme density across all verses. We then use this value to determine at which iteration this rhyme density is achieved during generation (using the regression line for rhyme density). Next, we use the maximum similarity regression to determine the maximum similarity score at that iteration. Low maximum similarity score indicates that we have maintained stylistic similarity while producing new, previously unseen lyrics.

Note that the reason for negative numbers in Table 3 is that in the beginning of training (in case of LSTM) and at a low n-gram length (for the baseline model), the models actually achieved a rhyme density that exceeded the artist's average rhyme density. As a result, the rhyme density regression line hits the average rhyme density on a negative iteration.

7 Discussion

In order to understand better the interaction between the four metrics we have introduced in this paper, we examined correlation coefficients between different measures of quality for generated verse (see Table 4). The lack of strong correlation supports the notion that different aspects of verse quality should be addressed separately and are, in fact, complementary. Even the measures of *fluency* and *coherence*, despite sharing a similar goal, have a relatively low correlation of 0.4.

Interestingly, the number of verses a rapper has in our dataset has a strong negative correlation with coherence score (cf. Table 5). This can be explained by the following consideration: on iteration 16,000, the model for the authors with the smaller number of verses has seen the same verses more times than the model trained on a larger number of verses. Therefore, it is easier for the former to produce more coherent lyrics since it saw more of the same patterns. As a result, models trained on a larger number of verses have a lower coherence score. For example, Lil' Wayne has the most verses in our data, and correspondingly, the model for his verse has the worst coherence score. Note that the fluency score does not have this negative correlation with the number of verses. Based on our evaluation, 16,000 iterations is enough to learn a language model for the given artist that produces fluent lines. However, these lines will not necessarily form a coherent verse if the artist has a large number of verses. Furthermore, although the average fluency score was 0.723, which can be interpreted as being roughly halfway between weakly fluent and strongly fluent, the standard de-

Artist	Avg Rhyme Density	Baseline		LSTM	
		Similarity	N-gram	Similarity	iteration
Tupac	0.302	**0.024**	−2	0.065	−3168
Aesop Rock	0.349	0.745	7	**0.460**	12 470
DMX	0.341	0.663	6	**0.431**	8271
Drake	0.341	0.586	5	**0.519**	9949
Eminem	0.325	0.337	3	**0.302**	8855
Fabolous	0.360	1.353	14	**0.569**	14 972
GZA	0.280	**0.520**	4	0.616	14 939
Jay Z	0.365	0.499	5	**0.463**	15 147
Lil' Wayne	0.362	0.619	6	**0.406**	9249
Notorious B.I.G.	0.383	0.701	7	**0.428**	3723
Sage Francis	0.415	0.764	8	**0.241**	−187
Average	-	0.619	-	**0.409**	-

Table 3: The results of the automated evaluation. The bold indicates the system with a lower similarity at the target rhyme density.

	Coherence	Fluency	Similarity	Matching
Coherence	1.000	0.398	0.102	-0.285
Fluency	0.398	1.000	0.137	-0.276
Similarity	0.102	0.137	1.000	0.092
Matching	-0.285	-0.276	0.092	1.000

Table 4: The correlation between the four metrics we have developed: Coherence, Fluency, similarity score based on automated evaluation (Similarity), and Style Matching (Matching).

viation was 0.178. Referring to Table 5, we have yet to find a linguistic statistic that accounts for this variance in fluency score amoung the artists.

	Coherence	Fluency	Similarity	Matches
Verses	-0.509	-0.084	0.133	0.111
Tokens	-0.463	-0.229	-0.012	0.507
Vocab Richness	0.214	0.116	-0.263	0.107

Table 5: The correlation between the number of verses/tokens and average coherence, fluency, and similarity scores, as well as $Match_A\%$ at 16000 iterations.

As can be seen from Table 2, the $Match\%$ score suggests that the LSTM-generated verses are able to capture the style of the artist as well as the original verses. Furthermore, $Match_A\%$ is significantly higher for the LSTM model, which means that the annotators agreed on matching verses more frequently (see Figure 5 as well). We believe this means that the LSTM model, trained on all verses from a given artist, is able to capture the artist's "average" style, whereas authentic verses represent a random selection that are less likely, statistically speaking, to be similar to another random verse. One aspect to which the match results for authentic verse point is that practically, in terms of artist style, certain artists are more distinct, making them better suited to be target artists for the ghostwriting tasks. For example, GZA recorded the highest $Match\%$, $Match_A\%$, and agreement percentage, meaning his style is the most distinguishable. Note that as expected, there is a strong correlation between the number of tokens in the artist's data and the frequency of agreed-upon correct style matches (cf. Table 5). Since verses vary in length, this correlation is not observed for verses. Finally, the absence of strong correlation with vocabulary richness suggests that the uniqueness of the tokens themselves is not as important as the sheer volume.

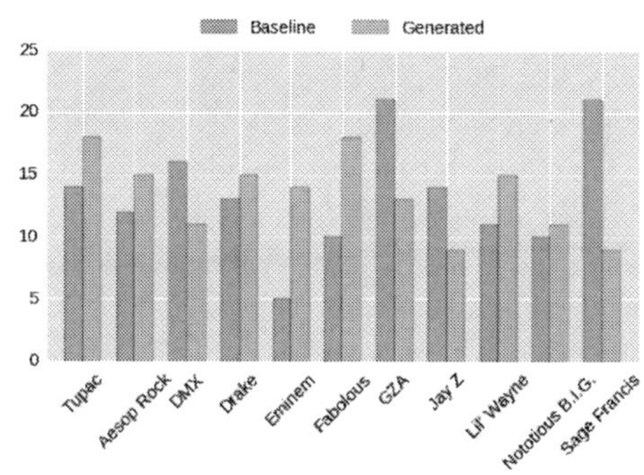

Figure 5: The numbers of style matches in the Style Matching evaluation. The maximum possible number is 40.

One aspect of the generated verse we have not discussed so far is the structure of the generated

Artist	Max Len	% of training completed
Tupac	454	69.7
Aesop Rock	450	91.0
DMX	361	64.9
Drake	146	82.3
Eminem	452	90.8
Fabolous	278	47.3
GZA	433	81.1
Jay Z	449	98.5
Lil' Wayne	253	92.7
Nototious B.I.G.	253	83.0
Sage Francis	280	53.9
Average	-	77.8

Table 6: The maximum lengths of generated verses and % of training completed on which the verse is generated

verse. For example, the length of the generated verses should be evaluated, since the models we examined do generate line breaks and also decide when to end the verse. Table 6 shows the longest verse generated for each artist, and also the point at which it was achieved during the training. We note that although 10 of the 11 models are able to generate long verses (up to a full standard deviation above the average verse length for that author), it takes a substantial amount of time, and the correlation between the average verse length for a given an artist and the verse length achieved by the model is weak (0.258). This suggests that modeling the specific verse structure, including length, is one aspect that should be better addressed in the future.

Lastly, we note that the fully automated methodology we propose is able to replicate the results of the previously available semi-automatic method for the rapper Fabolous, which was the only artist evaluated by Potash et al. (2015). Furthermore, the results of automated evaluation for the 11 artists confirm that the LSTM model generalizes better than the baseline model.

8 Conclusions and Future Work

In this paper, we have presented a comprehensive evaluation methodology for the task of ghostwriting rap lyrics, which captures complementary aspects of this task and its goals. We developed a manual evaluation method that assesses several key properties of generated verse, and created a data set of authentic verse, manually annotated for style matching. Previously proposed semi-automatic evaluation method has now been fully automated, and shown to replicate results of the original method. We have shown how the proposed evaluation methodology can be used to evaluate an LSTM-based ghostwriter model. We believe our evaluation experiments also clearly demonstrate that complementary evaluation methods are required to capture different aspects of the ghostwriting task.

Lastly, our evaluation provides key insights into future directions of the generative models themselves. For example, the automated evaluation shows how the LSTM's inability to integrate new vocabulary makes it difficult to achieve truly desirable similarity scores; future generative models can draw on the work of (Graves, 2013; Bowman et al., 2015) in an attempt to leverage other artists' lyrics.

References

Gabriele Barbieri, François Pachet, Pierre Roy, and Mirko Degli Esposti. 2012. Markov constraints for generating lyrics with style. In *ECAI*, pages 115–120.

Steven Bird, Ewan Klein, and Edward Loper. 2009. *Natural Language Processing with Python*. O'Reilly Media.

Samuel R Bowman, Luke Vilnis, Oriol Vinyals, Andrew M Dai, Rafal Jozefowicz, and Samy Bengio. 2015. Generating sentences from a continuous space. *arXiv preprint arXiv:1511.06349*.

Leon A Gatys, Alexander S Ecker, and Matthias Bethge. 2015. A neural algorithm of artistic style. *arXiv preprint arXiv:1508.06576*.

Pablo Gervás. 2000. Wasp: Evaluation of different strategies for the automatic generation of spanish verse. In *Proceedings of the AISB-00 Symposium on Creative & Cultural Aspects of AI*, pages 93–100.

Alex Graves. 2013. Generating sequences with recurrent neural networks. *arXiv preprint arXiv:1308.0850*.

Hussein Hirjee and Daniel Brown. 2010a. Using automated rhyme detection to characterize rhyming style in rap music.

Hussein Hirjee and Daniel G Brown. 2010b. Rhyme analyzer: An analysis tool for rap lyrics. In *Proceedings of the 11th International Society for Music Information Retrieval Conference*. Citeseer.

Chuan Li and Michael Wand. 2016. Combining markov random fields and convolutional neural networks for image synthesis. *arXiv preprint arXiv:1601.04589*.

Eric Malmi, Pyry Takala, Hannu Toivonen, Tapani Raiko, and Aristides Gionis. 2015. Dopelearning: A computational approach to rap lyrics generation. *arXiv preprint arXiv:1505.04771*.

Hugo Gonçalo Oliveira, Raquel Hervás, Alberto Díaz, and Pablo Gervás. 2014. Adapting a generic platform for poetry generation to produce spanish poems. In *5th International Conference on Computational Creativity, ICCC*.

Peter Potash, Alexey Romanov, and Anna Rumshisky. 2015. Ghostwriter: Using an LSTM for automatic rap lyric generation. In *Proceedings of the 2015 Conference on Empirical Methods in Natural Language Processing*.

Dekai Wu, Karteek Addanki, Markus Saers, and Meriem Beloucif. 2013. Learning to freestyle: Hip hop challenge-response induction via transduction rule segmentation. In *2013 Conference on Empirical Methods in Natural Language Processing (EMNLP 2013), Seattle, Washington, USA*.

Karteek Addanki Dekai Wu. 2014. Evaluating improvised hip hop lyrics–challenges and observations. In *LREC*.

A Appendix: Additional visualizations

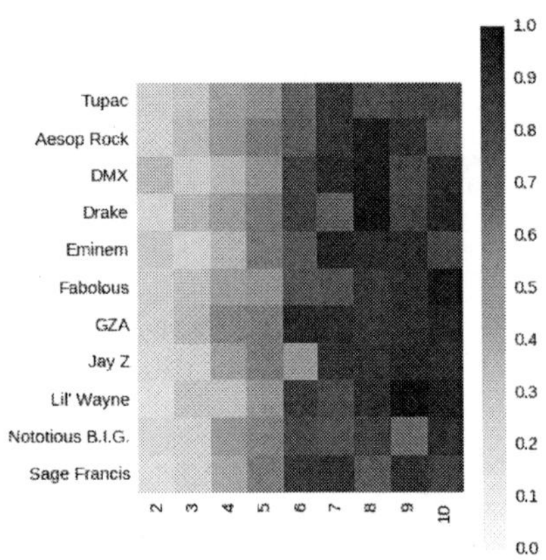

Figure 6: The maximum similarity score of the n-gram model by n.

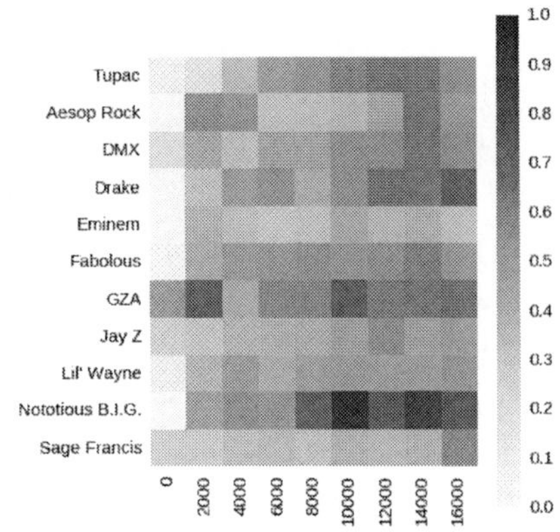

Figure 7: The maximum similarity score of the LSTM model by epoch. Note that LSTM model does not achieve as high a similarity as the n-gram model even on the latter epochs.

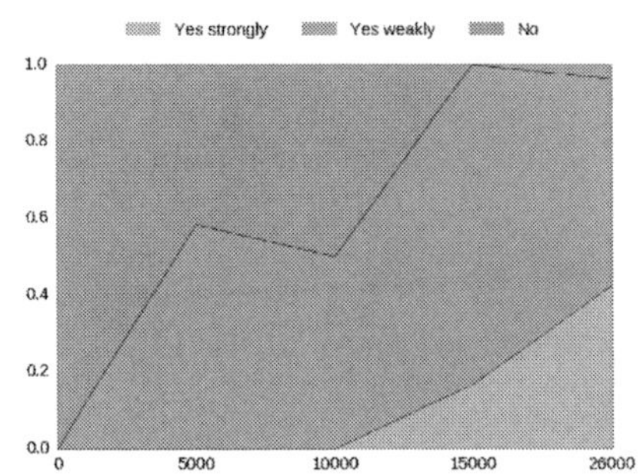

Figure 8: The training process of Fabolous in terms of fluency evaluation

Cross-corpus Native Language Identification via Statistical Embedding

Francisco Rangel
Universitat Politècnica de València
Valencia - Spain
francisco.rangel@autoritas.es

Paolo Rosso
Universitat Politècnica de València
Valencia - Spain
prosso@dsic.upv.es

Alexandra L. Uitdenbogerd
RMIT University
Melbourne - Australia
sandra.uitdenbogerd@rmit.edu.au

Julian Brooke
Thomson Reuters - Canada
julian.brooke@gmail.com

Abstract

In this paper, we approach the task of native language identification in a realistic cross-corpus scenario where a model is trained with available data and has to predict the native language from data of a different corpus. We have proposed a statistical embedding representation reporting a significant improvement over common single-layer approaches of the state of the art, identifying Chinese, Arabic, and Indonesian in a cross-corpus scenario. The proposed approach was shown to be competitive even when the data is scarce and imbalanced.

1 Introduction

Native Language Identification (NLI) is the task of identifying the native language (L1) of a writer based solely on a textual sample of their writing in a second language (L2), for example, essays in English by students from China, Indonesia or Arabic-speaking countries. NLI is very important for education, since it can lead to the provision of more targeted feedback to language learners about their most common errors. It is also of interest for forensics, security and marketing. For example, knowing the possible native language of the user who wrote a potentially threatening message may help to better profile that user and the potential scope of the threat.

The first Native Language Identification shared task was organised in 2013 (Tetreault et al., 2013). The twenty-nine teams had to classify essays written in English (L2) in one of the eleven possible native languages (L1). The most common features were word, character and POS n-grams, and the reported accuracies rose to 83.6%. The Support Vector Machine (SVM) has been the most prevalent classification approach. Furthermore, participants were allowed to train their models with external data, specifically *i)* any kind of external data, excluding TOEFL[1] (Blanchard et al., 2013); or *ii)* any kind of external data, including TOEFL. Participants such as Brooke and Hirst (Brooke and Hirst, 2013) combined data from sources such as Lang8,[2] ICLE[3] (Granger, 2003), FCE[4] (Yannakoudakis et al., 2011), and ICNALE[5] (Ishikawa, 2011). The reported accuracies show that, when training only with external data, the results fall to 56.5%. Recently, the 2017 Native Language Identification Shared Task (Malmasi et al., 2017) has been organised with the aim of identifying the native language of written texts, alongside a second task on spoken transcripts and low dimensional audio file representations as data (although original audio files were not shared). The organisers included the macro-averaged F1-score (Yang and Liu, 1999) since it evaluates the performance across classes more consistently. Although deep learning approaches were widely used, the best results (up to 88.18%) were achieved with classical methods such as SVM and n-grams. Despite participants being allowed to use external data, there were no such submissions, possibly also due to the poor results obtained in the previous edition (56.5% of accuracy).

We are interested in the following cross-corpus scenario: a model trained with data from external sources (e.g. social media). The authors in (Malmasi and Dras, 2015) used the EF Cambridge Open Language Database (EFCamDat)[6] (Geertzen et al., 2013) for training and

[1] https://www.ets.org/research/policy_research_reports/publications/report/2013/jrkv
[2] http://www.lang8.com
[3] https://uclouvain.be/en/research-institutes/ilc/cecl/icle.html
[4] https://ilexir.co.uk/datasets/index.html
[5] http://language.sakura.ne.jp/icnale/
[6] https://corpus.mml.cam.ac.uk/efcamdat1/

Proceedings of the 2nd Workshop on Stylistic Variation, pages 39–43
New Orleans, Louisiana, June 5, 2018.

TOEFL for evaluation, and vice versa. They trained a linear-SVM with several features such as function word unigrams and bigrams, production rules and part-of-speech unigrams, bigrams and trigrams, and the combination of all of them. The authors reported an accuracy of 33.45% when training with EFCamDat and evaluated on TOEFL, and an accuracy of 28.42% when training on TOEFL, and evaluated on EFCamDat, in contrast to the accuracy of 64.95% obtained when evaluating intra-corpus. The authors in (Ionescu et al., 2016) evaluated String Kernels in a cross-corpus scenario (TOEFL11 for training and TOEFL11-Big (Tetreault et al., 2012) for evaluation). They reported significant improvements over the state of the art with accuracies up to 67.7%. The authors explain these results by arguing "that string kernels are language independent, and for the same reasons they can also be topic independent".

In this work, we propose to follow the methodology represented in Figure 1. Given a set of corpora C, we learn a model with all the corpora together except c, which is used to evaluate the model. To evaluate the task, we have proposed a statistical embedding representation that we have compared with common single-layer approaches based on n-grams, obtaining encouraging results.

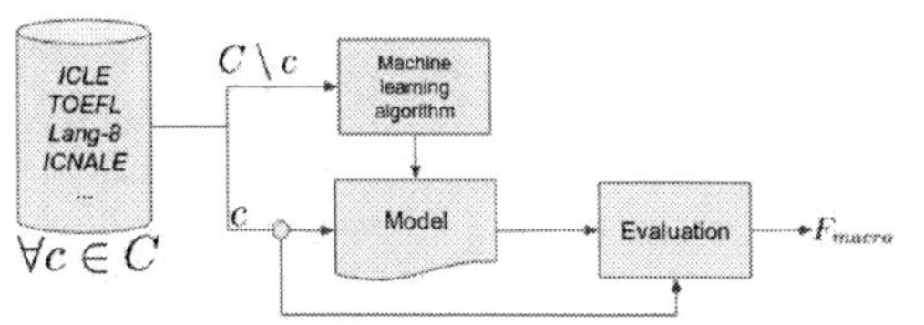

Figure 1: Evaluation methodology.

2 Corpora

Due to the typical geographical origins of students registered in Australian universities, our interest is in Arabic (AR), Chinese (CH) and Indonesian (ID). Arabic is incorporated in TOEFL and Lang8, as well as Chinese. Indonesian is included in Lang8 and ICNALE. The number of documents per corpus and language is shown in Table 1. As can be seen, classes are very imbalanced in most cases. Furthermore, in the case of Indonesian, figures for the ICNALE corpus are very small[7].

[7]We have used the merged text set from the ICNALE Written Essays 2.0

NL	Corpus	L1	Others
AR	Lang8	1,139	23,931
	TOEFL	1,103	10,997
CH	Lang8	22,549	16,102
	TOEFL	1,102	10,998
ID	Lang8	1,143	23,923
	ICNALE	8	74

Table 1: Number of documents in each corpus. *L1* corresponds to the documents written by authors of the native language to be identified. *Others* comprise all the documents written by authors of the other native languages in the corpus.

3 Low Dimensionality Statistical Embedding

As shown in (Brooke and Hirst, 2012; Ionescu et al., 2014), single-layer representations such as n-grams are able to obtain competitive results in a cross-corpus scenario. However, n-grams use to be filtered in order to reduce dimensionality, and generally the most frequent ones are selected. Nevertheless, omitting some of the rarest terms is fairly common and necessary for top performance. We propose a Low Dimensionality Statistical Embedding (LDSE) to represent the documents on the basis of the probability distribution of the occurrence of all their terms in the different languages, i.e. L1. Furthermore, LDSE represents texts without the need of using external resources or linguistic tools, nor preprocessing or feature engineering. The intuition is that the distribution of weights for a given document should be closer to the weights of its corresponding native language. The proposed representation relies on descriptive statistics to carry out the comparison among distributions. Formally, we represent the documents as follows.

We calculate the *tf-idf* weights for the terms in the training set D and build the matrix Δ. Each row represents a document d_i, each column a vocabulary term t_j, and each cell represents the *tf-idf* weight w_{ij} for each term in each document. Finally, $\delta(d_i)$ represents the assigned native language c to the document i.

$$\Delta = \begin{bmatrix} w_{11} & w_{12} & ... & w_{1m} & \delta(d_1) \\ w_{21} & w_{22} & ... & w_{2m} & \delta(d_2) \\ ... & ... & ... & ... & \\ w_{n1} & w_{n2} & ... & w_{nm} & \delta(d_n) \end{bmatrix}, \quad (1)$$

Eq. 2 shows how we obtain the term weights $W(t, c)$ as the ratio between the weights of the documents belonging to a given native language c

and the total distribution of weights for that term.

$$W(t,c) = \frac{\sum_{d \in D/c=\delta(d)} w_{dt}}{\sum_{d \in D} w_{dt}}, \forall d \in D, c \in C \quad (2)$$

As shown in Eq. 3, these term weights are used to obtain the representation of the documents.

$$d = \{F(c_1), F(c_2), ..., F(c_n)\} \sim \forall c \in C, \quad (3)$$

Each $F(c_i)$ contains the set of features showed in Eq. 4, with the following meaning: *i)* average and median values of the document term weights; *ii)* minimum and maximum values of the weights in the document; *iii)* first and third quartiles of the weights distribution; *iv)* Gini (Gini, 1912) indexes (to measure the distribution skewness and kurtosis); and *vi)* the nine first moments (Bowman and Shenton, 1985) (the more moments two distributions share, the more similar they are).

$$F(c_i) = \{avg, median, min, max, Q_1, Q_3, G_1, G_2, M_2, .., M_{10}\} \quad (4)$$

Finally, these weights are learned with a machine learning algorithm. We have tested several machine learning algorithms and we report the ones with the best results: *i)* Naive Bayes in Lang8 for Arabic and Indonesian, as well as in ICNALE for Indonesian; *ii)* Simple Logistic in TOEFL for Arabic; *ii)* SVM in TOEFL and Lang8 for Chinese; and *iii)* Neural Networks in the Student Writing Task (SWT) for the three languages.

As can be seen, this representation reduces the dimensionality to only 17 features per class by statistically embedding the distribution of weights of the document terms, but unlike methods such as PCA or LSA, it takes into account all the terms in the corpus instead of removing those ones that contribute less. We have evaluated several machine learning algorithms and reported the best results obtained.

We have used both character and word n-grams with SVM to compare our proposal since they are the most common features used in the state of the art. We have iterated n from 1 to 5 with the top 100, 500, 1,000 and 5,000 most frequent terms.

4 Experimental scenario

In this section we report and discuss the obtained results. Firstly, we focus on the described corpora for the languages of interest. Then, we analyse as a case study the Australian academic scenario. Due to the imbalance of the data, we use a macro-averaged F1-score which gives the same importance to the different classes no matter their size.

4.1 Results on NLI corpora

Although NLI has most commonly approached as multi-class, the difficulty lining up multiple languages across multiple corpora means that we instead focus here on the one versus all (1va) formulation; we note that in practice multi-class NLI using SVMs is of realized using 1va SVM classification (Brooke and Hirst, 2012), so our results here should extend directly to the multi-class case. Results are presented in Table 2. The second and third columns show respectively the corpus used for training and test: Lang8 and TOEFL include Arabic and Chinese, whereas Indonesian is included in Lang8 and ICNALE. The fourth column shows the best result obtained by the baseline:[8], whereas the fifth column shows the result obtained with LDSE.

NL	Train	Test	Base	LDSE	%
AR	Lang8	TOEFL	54.75	65.30	19.27
	TOEFL	Lang8	51.10	59.60	16.63
CH	Lang8	TOEFL	53.25	56.95	6.95
	TOEFL	Lang8	50.10	52.30	4.39
ID	Lang8	ICNALE	73.05	86.15	17.93
	ICNALE	Lang8	53.75	61.35	14.14

Table 2: Results in macro-averaged F1-score. The baseline corresponds to the best result obtained with character or word n-grams. The last column shows the improvement percentage achieved by LDSE over the baseline.

As can be seen, LDSE significantly[9] outperforms the best results obtained with n-grams for all languages and setups, with improvements from 4.39% up to to 19.27%. The highest improvement has been obtained for Arabic, although the best results were achieved for Indonesian. It is worth mentioning that, as shown in Table 1, the ICNALE corpus is very small: 8 documents for Indonesian and 74 documents for the other 9 native languages. Due to that, especially in the case of evaluating on ICNALE, a small variation in the identification can cause a high variability in the results.

[8]The best results have been obtained with the following setups *i)* character 5-grams; *ii)* word 1-grams; *iii)* character 4-grams; *iv)* character 4-grams; *v)* word 1-grams; *vi)* character 2-grams. In all the cases the 1,000 most frequent n-grams were selected.

[9]T-Student at 95% of significance was used.

Despite Chinese being larger and less imbalanced in Lang8 (as can be seen in Table 1), the overall results are lower and closer to the baseline. No matter the language, the best results have been obtained when training with Lang8. This may be due to the larger size of this dataset, and especially to the freedom of choice of their authors to write about different topics.

4.2 Case study

With the aim of investigating the performance of our approach in the Australian academic scenario, we have tested LDSE on the Student Writing Task (SWT) corpus for the three native languages and compared the results obtained for the previous corpora. SWT contains 32 essays of 200–300 words, written by Computer Science PhD students studying in Australia. The students had 16 different native languages, including: Arabic (4), Chinese (5), and Indonesian (4). The essays all discuss the same topic, being the relative merit of three algorithms.

To train our model, we have used Lang8 together with TOEFL in the case of Arabic and Chinese, and Lang8 with ICNALE in the case of Indonesian. No data from SWT was used for training.

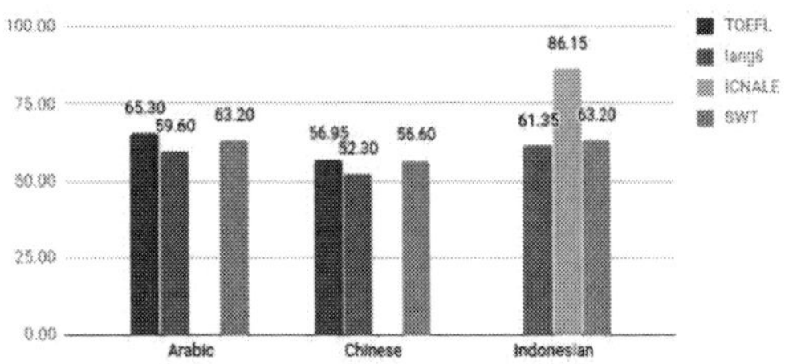

Figure 2: Comparative results of the LDSE model on the different corpora.

As shown in Figure 2, results on SWT are similar to those obtained on Lang8 and TOEFL on the three languages. Specifically, results obtained on TOEFL are slightly better, whereas they are slightly worse in the case of Lang8, without statistical significance in any case. However, results obtained on ICNALE are significantly higher.

5 Conclusions and future work

In this work, we have approached the task of identifying the native language of authors based on their written text in English, focussing on the languages of the main geographical origins of students in the Australian academic environment: Arabic, Chinese, and Indonesian.

We have proposed the LDSE statistical embedding approach that considers descriptive statistics such as the distribution skewness and kurtosis (Gini indexes) as well as the moment information to represent the documents of the three different classes (native languages). We have evaluated LDSE on the available corpora, showing a higher performance than SVM approaches based on n-grams that obtained the bests results in the NLI previous shared tasks. Finally, we have evaluated LDSE also on the written essays of the SWT case study, showing its competitiveness from a cross-corpus perspective despite the small size and imbalance degree of the corpus.

Although it is typical to treat NLI as a multi-class problem instead of 1-vs-all, the main difficulty would be to line up multiple languages across multiple corpora. Furthermore, our interest is in identifying whether the L1 is Arabic, Chinese or Indonesian. We aim to address NLI from multi-class perspective as a future work.

Acknowledgments

The research of the second author was partially funded by the SomEMBED TIN2015-71147-C2-1-P MINECO research project. The work on the data of authors whose native language is Arabic as well as this publication were made possible by NPRP grant #9-175-1-033 from the Qatar National Research Fund (a member of Qatar Foundation). The statements made herein are solely the responsibility of the first two authors.

References

Daniel Blanchard, Joel Tetreault, Derrick Higgins, Aoife Cahill, and Martin Chodorow. 2013. Toefl11: A corpus of non-native english. *ETS Research Report Series* 2013(2).

Kamiko O Bowman and Leonard R Shenton. 1985. Method of moments. *Encyclopedia of statistical sciences* 5:467–473.

Julian Brooke and Graeme Hirst. 2012. Robust, lexicalized native language identification. *Proceedings of COLING 2012* pages 391–408.

Julian Brooke and Graeme Hirst. 2013. Using other learner corpora in the 2013 nli shared task. In *Proceedings of the Eighth Workshop on Innovative Use of NLP for Building Educational Applications*. pages 188–196.

Jeroen Geertzen, Theodora Alexopoulou, and Anna Korhonen. 2013. Automatic linguistic annotation of large scale l2 databases: The ef-cambridge open language database (efcamdat). In *Proceedings of the 31st Second Language Research Forum. Somerville, MA: Cascadilla Proceedings Project*.

CW Gini. 1912. Variability and mutability, contribution to the study of statistical distribution and relaitons. *Studi Economico-Giuricici della R* .

Sylviane Granger. 2003. The international corpus of learner english: a new resource for foreign language learning and teaching and second language acquisition research. *Tesol Quarterly* 37(3):538–546.

Radu Tudor Ionescu, Marius Popescu, and Aoife Cahill. 2014. Can characters reveal your native language? a language-independent approach to native language identification. In *Proceedings of the 2014 Conference on Empirical Methods in Natural Language Processing (EMNLP)*. pages 1363–1373.

Radu Tudor Ionescu, Marius Popescu, and Aoife Cahill. 2016. String kernels for native language identification: Insights from behind the curtains. *Computational Linguistics* 42(3):491–525.

Shinichiro Ishikawa. 2011. A new horizon in learner corpus studies: The aim of the icnale project. *Corpora and language technologies in teaching, learning and research* pages 3–11.

Shervin Malmasi and Mark Dras. 2015. Large-scale native language identification with cross-corpus evaluation. In *Proceedings of the 2015 Conference of the North American Chapter of the Association for Computational Linguistics: Human Language Technologies*. pages 1403–1409.

Shervin Malmasi, Keelan Evanini, Aoife Cahill, Joel Tetreault, Robert Pugh, Christopher Hamill, Diane Napolitano, and Yao Qian. 2017. A report on the 2017 native language identification shared task. In *Proceedings of the 12th Workshop on Innovative Use of NLP for Building Educational Applications*. pages 62–75.

Joel Tetreault, Daniel Blanchard, and Aoife Cahill. 2013. A report on the first native language identification shared task. In *Proceedings of the eighth workshop on innovative use of NLP for building educational applications*. pages 48–57.

Joel Tetreault, Daniel Blanchard, Aoife Cahill, and Martin Chodorow. 2012. Native tongues, lost and found: Resources and empirical evaluations in native language identification. *Proceedings of COLING 2012* pages 2585–2602.

Yiming Yang and Xin Liu. 1999. A re-examination of text categorization methods. In *Proceedings of the 22nd annual international ACM SIGIR conference on Research and development in information retrieval*. ACM, pages 42–49.

Helen Yannakoudakis, Ted Briscoe, and Ben Medlock. 2011. A new dataset and method for automatically grading esol texts. In *Proceedings of the 49th Annual Meeting of the Association for Computational Linguistics: Human Language Technologies-Volume 1*. Association for Computational Linguistics, pages 180–189.

Author Index

Balusu, Murali Raghu Babu, 11
Brooke, Julian, 39

Degaetano-Ortlieb, Stefania, 1

Eisenstein, Jacob, 11

Hu, Hai, 20

Kübler, Sandra, 20

Li, Wen, 20

Merghani, Taha, 11

Potash, Peter, 29

Rangel, Francisco, 39
Romanov, Alexey, 29
Rosso, Paolo, 39
Rumshisky, Anna, 29

Uitdenbogerd, Alexandra, 39